Blessin,
Michelle
Thomas

Debt-Free Living in a Debt-Filled World

A book to encourage, educate, inform, and inspire.

Michelle Thomas

with Trevor Grant Thomas

Readers should be aware that Internet websites mentioned as references or sources for further information may have changed or no longer be available since this book was published.

Published by Michelle Thomas

ISBN ePub: 978-0-9911291-1-9
ISBN paperback: 978-0-9911291-0-2

Retail price $15.99

Editing by James Armstrong and Jane Kesler

Cover design by Sean Allen

Consultation by Kevin Light, Lighten Media Group

Cover photography by Joanna Henderson

Scripture quotations are taken from the HOLY BIBLE, NEW INTERNATIONAL VERSION. Copyright 1973, 1978, 1984 by International Bible Society.

To purchase this book for trade distribution, go to Amazon.com. To contact the publisher, go to www.KingdomCrossing.com.

201404V2

DEDICATION

This book is dedicated to my Lord and Savior, Jesus Christ. You are my All in All, my Redeemer, my Best Friend, and my Bridegroom for all eternity. Without You, I am nothing.

CONTENTS

ACKNOWLEDGMENTS

First and foremost, I want to thank the Lord for creating me and for giving me life. Without Him, this story wouldn't have happened. He has protected, guided, and blessed our family through thick and thin. He brought us together and gave us His wisdom on each step of our journey. Thank You, Lord, for being awesome and mighty!

Without my dear husband's sensitive spirit, my life would've taken a dramatically different path. Because he heard the Lord and obeyed, our family has been blessed in a multitude of ways. Thank you, Trevor, for your encouragement, support, hard work, faithfulness, and for all of your help and input with this book. Thank you for making me laugh, for giving me a house full of rambunctious little blessings, and for guiding our family closer to the Lord each day.

Thank you, thank you, thank you to everyone who toiled and labored as we were constructing our house. You partnered with us in something amazing and wonderful, even if you didn't know it at the time. I'm not sure if I can remember everyone, but here's a try: Mom and Dad, Edsel and Carolyn, Ernest, Granny and Pa, Chris, Uncle Charlie, Larry, Benny, Mike, Aron, Don, Hoyt, Jeremy, Bob, Brad, Kim, and Michael.

Thank you to Jim Armstrong for being an amazing consultant, editor, and friend. I know that I bugged you to death with all of my questions, but you were so patient with me. Your wisdom has been invaluable. Thank you to Kevin Light for your direction in publishing and marketing. You are a life-long friend, and I'm blessed to know you. To Jane Kesler, I appreciate all of your thoughtful edits more than you will ever know. Thank you from the bottom of my heart.

To my sister-in-law, Jenn Fitzpatrick, thank you for all of your guidance and information regarding publishing and marketing. To Sean Allen, the best graphic designer in the world, thank you for your patience and hard work. Thank you to Mike Taylor, to my dad, to Carolyn Mitchell, and to my uncle Roger for reviewing the book and for giving me valuable feedback.

Finally, I want to thank my babies: Caleb, Jesse, Caroline, and Noah. You are my sunshine. You keep me humble. You pick flowers for me. You encourage me. You love me even when I'm unlovable. You give me a reason to get up each day. I love you with all my heart.

FOREWORD

As I have pondered the topic of finances as related to the Christian community, I can only imagine the magnitude of good that could be accomplished around the world if only God's people were free to live and give as they would like. What could the average Christian accomplish if he or she didn't have credit card debt or a mortgage payment or a car loan or student loans? Would we support the work of missionaries who are helping children in third-world countries? Would we travel abroad ourselves, sharing the Good News of Christ with those who haven't heard? Could we afford to educate our children in schools that would teach them from a godly worldview so they will withstand the pressures of the ever-darkening culture in which we live? Would we give of our time and resources regularly to help "the least of these" in our communities?

During my time at the helm of the Family Research Council, I came face to face with the pressures and struggles of Christians. They want to get in the trenches of the cultural war that is raging in this nation; they want to be on the front lines of the battle for the hearts and souls of our children; they want to take a stand in ways that will make a difference. However, so many of us are overwhelmed by financial pressures that we feel trapped and unable to step out and get involved.

With practical suggestions and lighthearted wisdom, Michelle and Trevor Thomas will steer you through the uncomfortable waters of debt and budgeting and stewardship. They will encourage you to live differently than the world so that you will become free to follow the path that God has shown you.

As our nation plunges further into debt and despair, may we become a beacon of hope and an example of financial faithfulness to those in our sphere of influence. As Mother Theresa once said, "In this life we cannot do great things. We can only do small things with great love." As we walk out of financial bondage into financial freedom, we will be released to do our part to change the world, one small act of love at a time.

In Christ,

Ken Connor, J.D.

President of Family Research Council 2000-2003

Co-Founder, Chairman of Center for a Just Society/John Jay Institute 2005-present

Author of *Sinful Silence*

Debt-Free Living in a
Debt-Filled World

1

HUMBLE BEGINNINGS

"And my God will meet all your needs according to his glorious riches in Christ Jesus." (Philippians 4:19)

It's interesting how our beginnings work to shape us into the kind of people we become as adults. That's certainly the case in my life. My parents both grew up with relatively little in the way of material wealth. My dad's dad was a public school teacher, back when teachers made considerably less than they do now. Dad's mom (as did most moms in those days) stayed home and, among many other things, raised five children. My mom's parents were missionaries, so my mom grew up in Nigeria, West Africa. Of course, missionary life presents a myriad of challenges, and a small income is one of them.

After their first year of college, my parents married in 1969; both were 18. They had my older brother a couple of years later. I was born next, in November 1973 in Griffin, Georgia. Both of my parents had to drop out of college to work, so they struggled in low-wage jobs as they had two, then three, then four children. I remember that we never had much money. My parents always struggled to make ends meet. One of my earliest memories is of being put in the car in what seemed like the middle of the night to go with Mom to pick up my dad from work. They shared one car, and often that meant living with inconveniences.

Oh, my parents tried. They worked hard. My mom was a secretary most of my growing up years. What do they call that now—Administrative Assistant? Later when I was in high school, she went back to college to finish her degree. In fact, when I started college, my older brother and Mom were also college students. Mom got her bachelor's degree in human resources management when I was 19 and is now a very successful HR manager for a world-wide manufacturing company. I'm very proud of her!

When I was young, my dad worked hard and finished his bachelor's degree and went on to obtain a master's degree in counseling. He became a pastor when I was 10. He was a middle school teacher for a brief time and has been a counselor and pastor for many years now, using his talents to minister to families and to the Body of Christ in Northeast Georgia.

Along with my parents' college degrees, however, came large student loans and not much in the way of pay increases early on. It was expensive to raise four children. My siblings and I were all involved in sports, band, and the many activities that keep children busy, so there were countless fees to be paid, instruments to be purchased, uniforms, school pictures, track shoes, tennis rackets, and food….oh, the food required to feed four growing bodies!

As life became more expensive, the credit card debt began to pile up, on top of the student loans and the car loans. I remember that my parents always seemed to be stressed about money. It was uncomfortable growing up in that type of environment, but on the bright side, it gave me a firm resolve to live differently when I was grown. Even before I knew God's principles for handling money, I had a sense of the weight that debt placed on a person. I developed very frugal habits, always looking for the best deals, working hard, and saving money as I was able.

I started my first job when I was 10. We had just moved to Hoschton, Georgia—to my dad's first pastorate. From then on I grew up a preacher's kid. The little church needed someone to clean each week, so I took the job. I was paid $6 a week for several years, and then I was excited to have my "salary" raised to $7 a week! I was paid once a month, and I was always so happy to get my check, give 10 percent back to the church for my tithe, and spend the rest on things that I wanted—usually new clothes.

We had always depended on hand-me-downs for clothing. I guess I was thankful for them; I really don't remember. I do know that it was exciting to go through the bags of clothes that people gave us, but there was something extra special about working hard and buying my own brand new clothes. I continued to clean our church for most of the eight years that we were at the Hoschton church. As I entered my teen years, I babysat a lot, I worked occasionally as a waitress at a local restaurant, I ran a miniature golf course one summer, and when I was old enough, I did office work at the local Mitsubishi plant where my mom worked. All of these jobs helped tremendously to solidify my work ethic, give me the financial independence that I wanted, and provide for the extras that go along with being a young adult.

Having enough vehicles for a growing family was a challenge for my parents. During my high school years, my parents often allowed me to drive one of their vehicles back and forth to school, sports practice, and work, which I realize now was quite a sacrifice for them. One of us always took my mom to work and picked her up during those years, so she did without a car much of the time. At the end of high school, I was blessed to purchase a tiny Daihatsu car. My parents co-signed a small loan for me at our local bank, which I later learned is strongly discouraged in Scripture, but I worked hard and paid it off quickly. How I enjoyed driving my little car that I affectionately named Betsy! I remember that I was able to fill up that little car for $7 or $8 a week. That's unheard of with today's gas prices.

There was always an expectation in our family that my siblings and I would go to college. I had no worries back then about how expensive college would be or how I would pay for it. Ignorance is bliss, as they say. Thankfully, I made good grades in high school (it was hard not to when making anything below an A on my report card would've gotten me grounded). Back then, there was a scholarship program sponsored by the governor that provided full tuition college scholarships for the valedictorian and salutatorian in each Georgia public high school. I worked and scrapped my way to graduate second in my high school class, so I was fortunate to earn a free ride scholarship to college. Also, because of our family size and financial situation, I received some

Pell grant money that helped with college expenses. During my second year in college, Georgia legalized a lottery, which funded a state-wide scholarship known as the Hope Scholarship. I qualified for the Hope Scholarship, which provided a full tuition scholarship plus several hundred dollars each quarter for books. I made a nice little profit to attend college.

I graduated high school and started at Gainesville College in the fall of 1992. I took full loads straight through, graduating with an associate of science degree in elementary education in just a year and a half. A brief experience at a public elementary school that was required for my degree revealed to me rather quickly that teaching other people's children was not in my future. I transferred the next quarter to North Georgia College, where I also took full loads every quarter and finished my bachelor's degree in sociology a year and a half later. I graduated summa cum laude as valedictorian of my college class in June 1995. (There were actually three valedictorians that year, so I wasn't alone.) I know this sounds crazy, but I took classes one extra quarter and extended my graduation so that I could get my scholarships one more time.

When I started college in 1992, I took a part-time job at a local bookstore to provide some spending money. I worked there for nearly a year and a half. When my school load became too heavy for the hours that I was required to work, I gave up the job to concentrate on my studies. After I transferred to North Georgia College, I took a job as a secretary at a small counseling center. I was needed only a few hours a week and didn't make much money, but some of the things that I learned through that experience have proved invaluable to me through the years. Maybe most importantly, my boss, Ronnie Weeks, introduced me to budgeting. I would watch as he made copies of his account pages from his budget workbook, and I asked him how it worked. He helped me understand how to create a budget, which would have a profound impact on my life going forward.

When I graduated from North Georgia College, Ronnie hired me as a medical social worker through his contract with a local home health agency. I made home visits to patients in five counties across Northeast Georgia, helping to connect them with services that they needed, praying with them during difficulties, and getting to know many of them like family. Most of my patients were elderly, and aside from a few who were really creepy, they were amazing people with amazing stories. One lady in her 90s gave me a pair of slippers that she had made by hand. Another lady gave me a beautiful porcelain house figurine that I still display today. One lady, in particular, made such an impact on me that I visited her even after I left the job. I rode in an ambulance to the hospital with a lady who was so discouraged with her life that she wanted to end it. I grew and matured more than I can describe during that time. The long car rides alone around beautiful Northeast Georgia gave me time to think and pray and hear from the Lord, and the experiences with those precious people changed me for the better. I will treasure the memories always.

After two years of doing social work, an opportunity arose to go to work for Larry Burkett's ministry, Christian Financial Concepts (CFC). I went for an interview, and by the time I got back to my office, CFC was calling to offer me the job. I jumped at the chance. I had used Larry's materials to develop my personal budget, and I had already begun to develop a passion for learning and living by God's principles for handling money. I was offered more money than I was currently making to take the job (a whopping $19,500!), and I was thankful to be offered group health insurance, since I had been paying for a policy on my own.

At Christian Financial Concepts, I was stationed in the Research and Response department. We were tasked with responding to letters and phone calls on Larry's behalf, so we had to study his writings, listen to his radio programs, and learn what he would say to people. I began to soak up God's financial principles like a sponge. Larry was an amazing man of God—so gifted, so wise, and so compassionate. I would listen to him answer questions on the radio that he had answered a thousand times before, but he made each caller feel like he or she was the most important person in the world at that moment.

Larry was sick with cancer when I started working at CFC in August 1997. He had been through surgeries to remove his kidney and his shoulder blade, and each time a new tumor would pop up, he would go through an experimental treatment to have it eradicated, as well. He lived in constant pain, but you wouldn't know it by the way he treated people. I so enjoyed those years of being in the presence of one I consider to be truly a Mighty Man of God.

The Lord used my rather humble beginnings to mold

and shape my personality, my character, and my spirit. Because I grew up with little financially, I became frugal as a young adult. I saw God's faithful hand of provision during my childhood, so I learned to trust Him as my Provider. I saw generosity modeled by my parents in spite of their lack, so I was inspired to be generous with what I had. (I'm happy to report that my parents learned about God's principles for handling money shortly after I left home; they worked diligently to pay off all of their consumer debt and now have only a small mortgage left.)

I'll share with you the story of how my husband and I met in the next chapter, but I want to tell you now about how his financial background shaped him. Born in 1969, Trevor is the oldest of three children. His dad Edsel served five years in the Navy before he met Trevor's mom Carolyn. Edsel then came home to settle down back in Northeast Georgia where his family lived. Trevor's parents were from neighboring counties, White and Habersham. They had Trevor when they were 20 and 25. They had no formal education or training, but Trevor's dad was fortunate to be hired with the Georgia Department of Transportation, where he worked his entire career. Trevor's mom worked in various jobs throughout the years.

Thankfully, Trevor's paternal grandparents owned a lot of land. They deeded a small lot to Trevor's parents, where they built their home. They built a basement first and lived there until they could finish the upstairs. They financed a small amount to build their home, around $15,000, and they paid off their loan ahead of schedule. Edsel grew up farming, so he and Carolyn have always had a nice-sized vegetable garden along with many varieties of fruit trees. Throughout their marriage, they have often planted enough to sell some of the extra at the local farmers' market. Some of Trevor's earliest memories involve harvesting big crops of turnips with many members of his dad's extended family and taking a fun overnight trip to the Atlanta Farmers' Market. Carolyn also taught me a bit about canning, and one of the ways that we helped our food budget early in our marriage was to can and preserve plenty of home-grown garden vegetables. Edsel and Carolyn have always been generous with their fruits and vegetables, and our family, along with many others, have been blessed by this generosity.

Trevor's parents are hard workers and always have been relatively frugal. They never purchased new vehicles until after they retired. When Trevor was old enough to drive, he drove his dad's 1965 pickup truck back and forth to school, work, and football practice. Trevor worked his first paying job during the summer when he was 14. He worked with his uncle Benny, whom they called "Pop," installing in-ground swimming pools. Much of Trevor's work included operating a shovel and a wheelbarrow. He would push wheelbarrows full of dirt or concrete over and over again, struggling under the weight of it. He was almost as skinny as a shovel back then. Later, Trevor worked at a convenience store for a couple of years. The store had a car wash, and sometimes he shoveled out the pits that collected the dirt and grime. It was a nasty job, but it was a job. He also stocked the shelves and coolers and later was entrusted with the cash register. At the end of high school and during college, Trevor worked at a golf course, a resort, a grocery store, and a few other places.

With this variety of experience, Trevor developed good people skills and an appreciation for hard work.

Trevor was a good student and made pretty good grades in high school. He knew that college was in his future, but he had little real direction about what he was supposed to do with his life. His elementary school aspiration was to be a wide-receiver for the Dallas Cowboys, but that didn't quite pan out. His mom worked hard to help him apply for financial aid, and he finished college with very little debt. At first, he pursued an engineering degree because of his skills in math and science, later switching to a degree in physics with a minor in mathematics. The challenge then was finding a job after graduation. What does one do with a physics degree in Northeast Georgia? Trevor was not seeking the Lord's direction very earnestly with regard to finding a career, so he ended up working in the lab at a local mining company, making a low wage and putting in long hours. The owners were difficult employers, and he hated the job.

During this time, Trevor spent several years teaching Sunday School at his church. It was this experience that brought him to the place where he felt God calling him to become a teacher. He quit his job, moved back in with his parents, and began working on a master's degree in math education at North Georgia College. A year into his graduate studies, Trevor was hired to teach mathematics at Gainesville High School. While working at the high school, he finished his master's degree and then pursued and completed a specialist degree at the University of Georgia in math education. These advanced degrees early in Trevor's career moved him quickly up Georgia's teacher pay scale. For us it was a blessing that all of his graduate studies were done prior to our marrying and having children.

Though Trevor grew up with similar beginnings as I, without much in the way of financial resources, he went the opposite direction as an adult. He wanted more. He didn't like being frugal, so he went into debt for the things that he wanted. As a young adult, he bought a brand new car; he ran up credit card debt; he bought many things that he didn't really need. He was also still renting and had nothing saved toward a home or anything else for that matter. Former Governor Zell Miller had made increasing Georgia's teachers' salaries a priority, but when we met five years into Trevor's career, he had nothing financially to show for his earnings.

Trevor and I gleaned valuable financial lessons from our parents, and God weaved those principles into the tapestry that is our lives today. Thinking of this reminds me of what Paul said in Romans 8:28, "And we know that in all things God works for the good of those who love him, who have been called according to his purpose." I'm thankful that this has been true in our lives.

Fortunately, God typically puts opposites together. As Larry Burkett used to say often, if a husband and wife both are savers or spenders, one of them is unnecessary. I had become a saver, and Trevor had developed a spender mentality. As a team, we would figure out how to complement each other in our strengths and compensate for each other's weaknesses. The Lord knows what He's doing!

2

KNIGHT IN SHINING ARMOR

"He who finds a wife finds what is good and receives favor from the Lord." (Proverbs 18:22)

Rewind to early 1996. I was still doing social work for the home health agency and enjoying life, yet I was longing for my soul mate. I had dated several people through the years, but with each one I had doubts in my spirit—an "icky" feeling that he just wasn't "Mr. Right." I dated some great guys over the years. One was an officer at the Naval Academy in Annapolis; one was head of technology at a local college; two were engineers-in-training at Georgia Tech; one, a police officer; one, a chef. All of them were believers, all, really nice men, but they weren't right for me—they weren't "my" knight.

In January 1997, I went to Brazil on a mission trip with my church as part of the worship team, and we had learned a number of worship songs in Portuguese. It was amazing to lead worship in an unfamiliar language and listen to the precious Brazilian Christians worship our Lord in their own way. It was an awesome time of ministry, and I felt God's presence on that trip more profoundly than ever before. I fell more deeply in love with Jesus, and I wanted everything that He wanted for my life. When I returned home, I knew that I had had enough of dating the wrong people. I wanted to get serious about getting ready for my future husband. I knew in my spirit that the Lord had someone in mind for me; I just couldn't understand why He was taking so long to bring him to me. I was 23 at the time, and people were beginning to wonder why I wasn't married yet. Even my sweet grandfather told me that maybe I was being too picky! I knew that the second most important decision in my life was choosing the man I would marry. The first, of course, was my decision to follow Christ. I didn't want to make a mistake in such a monumental part of my life, for marrying the "wrong" person could prove to be disastrous, as it has for many, many people.

I had heard about a book called *Knight in Shining Armor*. It was written for young ladies, and it presented a six-month plan for preparing oneself to be married—to get ready for one's knight. It involved a six-month break from dating, while memorizing Scriptures related to character issues that I wanted to work on in myself, reading Christian self-help books, and generally getting to know Jesus better. In order to be the best wife that I could be, I needed to be wholly and completely in love with Jesus first. After all, He is my ultimate bridegroom, and I will be His bride for eternity (Revelation 19:7).

The character issues that I focused on eliminating with my Scripture memorization cards were anger and careless words, a critical, judgmental spirit, and greed. I found verses related to those areas, wrote them on index cards, and worked on committing them to memory. Memorizing God's Word gives us such power against the schemes of the enemy. I can't say that I changed completely through the disciplines that I developed or the Scriptures that I memorized, but I like to think that God used that time to mold me a little more into the image of His Son.

I had prayed during my dating hiatus that the first man who asked me out after my six-months were up would be "the" one. Six months later in June 1997, I was finishing my six-month commitment of no dating, spending time getting to know the Lord better, and preparing myself for my knight. One of my co-workers at the counseling center where I worked as a social worker—we'll call him Josh—was married to a math teacher at a local high school. Josh came to work one day and told me that he wanted to introduce me to one of his wife's fellow math teachers, a guy named Trevor Thomas. Josh brought a yearbook to work to show me Trevor's picture. I thought he looked intriguing, so I asked several questions about him. I would send questions through my co-worker's wife to find out things about him. Then with my permission, his wife gave Trevor my phone number.

Trevor soon called me, and we chatted for awhile. I learned that he was a Christian, which was number one on my list of qualifications for a husband. He was smart, which was high on the list as well. He didn't drink or smoke—two more items checked off my list. So far, so good.

Besides teaching math, Trevor also coached football and track at his high school. After we talked awhile, he asked if he could meet me; I'm sure he wanted to see if he liked what he saw, but I refused, telling him that I wanted to talk more before we met in person. You see, I wanted to hear from the Lord—before I even met Trevor—to receive confirmation that Trevor was, indeed, my knight in shining armor. I believe I received that confirmation as we talked by phone several times over the next couple of weeks. I finally agreed to meet Trevor in person. On the last day of June, 1997, Trevor came to my office to meet me. We then traveled separately to TCBY (The Country's Best Yogurt) and had frozen yogurt together while we chatted. Of course, I didn't share with Trevor at the time what the Lord had shown me, but he would know it soon enough.

Trevor is about four-and-a-half years older than I. He was 27 when we met, and he was sick of the dating scene as well. He desperately wanted to be married and felt that God had someone for him. Trevor admittedly spent much time and energy looking for that special someone, but he was not really allowing God to guide him in the tremendous decision of whom to marry.

About three months after we first met, on October 7, 1997, I had an engagement ring on my finger, which ironically, I would later discover Trevor had financed completely. Four months after that, Trevor added a wedding band. In a whirlwind romance, the Lord brought two together as one, and thus began our journey together as a family.

3

BROKE

*"The rich rule over the poor, and the borrower is servant
to the lender." (Proverbs 22:7)*

Our wedding was the last day of January in 1998. We
married at my church, The Atlanta Vineyard Christian Fellowship, in Dunwoody. It was a beautiful day. For January,
it was warm, and everything was perfect. I couldn't sleep
well the night before, so I got up early and did aerobics to
burn off some nervous energy. When everyone else got up,
my dad made us all his famous oatmeal, with a big puddle of
butter in the middle and a pile of sugar on top of that.
Mmmmm.

The wedding was nice, other than a few minor glitches.

OUR WEDDING DAY, JANUARY 31, 1998.

The church had as-
signed a sound man
for our service whom
I had never seen be-
fore, and I'm not sure
that he had any train-
ing in running sound.
I had chosen several
songs to be played
during the service, and he kept messing up the order of the
songs or waiting *way* too long to start the songs. I had asked

that the Hallelujah Chorus be played at the end when Trevor and I were pronounced husband and wife and when we were walking down the aisle out of the sanctuary. I thought that was fitting, since it had taken us so long to find each other. The sound guy finally got it playing about the time we were outside of the church. He also had something strange going on with the sound system that made loud pops erupt all through the ceremony.

My pastor who married us had mononucleosis at the time, so he wasn't thinking very clearly and left out the part where we were to exchange rings (kind of important, right?). We whispered a reminder, so he added it before the ceremony ended. I had secretly recorded a song for Trevor that was to be played during the lighting of the unity candle, but Trevor was so distracted because of the rings that he hardly paid attention to my song. Oh well. Such is life. We made it through the wedding, smiled for pictures, hugged our friends and loved ones good-bye, and took off as a clueless young married couple, embarking on a journey that would take so many surprising twists and turns.

On our wedding night, we stayed at the Château Élan resort in Braselton. We found out that the place where we had made reservations for the rest of our honeymoon was closed down due to a snow storm, so we decided to go to Asheville, North Carolina, instead, which also had received a fair amount of snow the week before. The mountains were beautiful, but travel was limited. Snow, ice, and freezing temperatures abounded. We played game after game of Uno, saw the movie *Titanic* at the theater, and talked a lot about money. Trevor had been fairly evasive about his financial situation while we were dating—not that I pointedly asked him all of the details, but he wasn't quick to volunteer them, either. We had gotten some good Christian pre-marital counseling during our engagement, something I strongly recommend to all engaged couples, but we hadn't focused much on finances. Things moved so quickly that we didn't take the time, nor did we really want to discuss financial issues. It was more pleasant to keep them buried during the excitement of planning a wedding. There would be plenty of time to focus on money issues later. What I sadly realized while cooped up in our hotel room in Asheville, North Carolina, was that we were very broke and very much in debt.

I had scraped together every cent of my money to pay for our wedding—right at $3,000—so I knew that I didn't have anything to add to the mix. I had cashed out my small savings bonds, used my "retirement" fund—an envelope to which I had been adding $5 a week, and used every cent of income that I had made during the months that we were planning the wedding. Trevor revealed on the honeymoon that he didn't have any money either. It was then that I discovered that he had even financed my engagement ring with a high-interest finance company.

As if the stress of a wedding and all that goes along with a young marriage weren't enough, being broke and in a lot of debt were added to the equation. We took stock of our obligations and realized that we were around $25,000 in debt. That might not seem like much today, but on my gross salary of $19,500 and Trevor's salary of around $40,000, along with renting an apartment and having nothing in savings, it seemed like a huge mountain. This might sound crazy, but in light of this frank discussion about our financial situation, we made the decision to come home from our honeymoon two days early. We were able to get our money back from the hotel for those two days and save the money we would've spent eating out and sight-seeing. I was ready to get to work on a plan for paying off the debt.

The only debt that I brought into the marriage was for my car. When I was working as a social worker before CFC, I had purchased an older, used Taurus from a friend because Betsy, my little Daihatsu, was wearing out. The company had stopped making Daihatsu cars, so parts were difficult to find. Unfortunately, the used Taurus that I bought to replace my beloved Daihatsu turned out to be a big fat lemon. I had paid cash for the car, and immediately I began to have problems with it. I poured nearly $2,000 into repairing the car, and after some months decided it wasn't worth all of the expense to maintain it, and the gas mileage was terrible compared to my little Daihatsu. Just after I met Trevor, I made the decision to purchase a two-year-old Toyota Corolla that

I found at a local dealership. I got a $9,000 loan from my bank for the car at 10 percent interest—the one and only loan I ever obtained on my own. As I look back now, it's interesting that I was able to borrow so much money on my own despite my low salary. I'm surprised that the bank didn't require a co-signer. My payments were around $228 per month. I wasn't happy about having that much debt, but after pouring everything that I had into the lemon, I felt that I had little choice. The Corolla was a good, reliable car that got excellent gas mileage and served us very well until we outgrew it years later. By the way, we sold that Corolla to my sister and her husband seven years after I bought it, and it is still going strong today, at 18 years old and over 300,000 miles! God has blessed that little car, indeed.

While we were dating, Trevor had bought a piece of land north of Gainesville at a really good price ($6,900) to try to sell later as an investment. He had financed the land, so in addition to the loan on the land, he brought several other debts to the marriage: the loan on my engagement ring ($1,300), the loan on his vehicle ($5,500), some credit card debt ($2,000), and a small student loan ($300), to bring us to almost $25,000 of debt.

What I've come to realize over the years is that our beginnings were like so many young couples in the U.S. today. Millions of young Americans begin their marriages in the same debt trap we found ourselves. Student loans, automobile loans, credit card debt—these three things, along with home mortgages, have placed many young American couples in a high-stress situation very early in their marriage.

It's little wonder then that financial stress, or money troubles, has been one of the leading causes of divorce in the U.S. for decades now. I was determined that we were *not* going to allow our marriage to be a target because of debt.

4

HOW TO MANAGE YOUR MONEY

"Commit to the Lord whatever you do, and your plans will succeed." (Proverbs 16:3)

Shortly after the wedding, I asked Trevor to work through the *How to Manage Your Money* Bible study with me. It consisted of VHS recordings of Larry Burkett delivering his workshop to a group of people in Dahlonega, Georgia. There were six tapes, two sessions on each tape. Along with the set was a workbook for us to record notes and answers to the study questions.

I love so much what Larry had to say in the Introduction to the study that I think it's worth quoting here:

"This study is provided to help Christians understand God's attitude about *wealth*. There is so much religious 'folklore' in the financial realm that few Christians understand what is from God's Word and what is not.

"Having taught this subject in many Bible studies, I know what a revelation it is for most Christians to discover how much God does care about money.

"There are approximately 700 direct references to money in the Bible and hundreds more indirect references. Nearly two-thirds of all the parables Christ left us deal with the use of *money*. You will discover, as you progress through this study, that God equates our use of wealth with our commitment to Him.

"I hope that as a result of this study you will experience absolute peace in the area of finances, for that is what God promises. Do not wait until you finish the entire study to apply God's principles. As you recognize a need, apply God's cure. Share these principles with others and discuss them freely.

"Too long we have pretended that Christians have no financial problems. That is nonsense. We are subject to the same temptations as the nonbeliever. It is only through God's blessings that we can escape from those snares. But how can we experience His blessing if we don't understand His plan? We cannot; therefore, this study will focus on God's plan exclusively."[1]

Wow. That was exactly what we needed—"absolute peace in the area of finances." We watched the workshop together over a couple of weeks' time, each recording notes and answers in the workbook. Trevor was so inspired by what he had heard that he went through the study again on his own. I think that I could've told him about those same biblical financial principles until I was blue in the face (and I probably already had, to some degree), but hearing Larry deliver them, along with the many references to Scripture that Larry employed, gripped Trevor's heart and he was changed forever. Larry had a way of reaching people with

---

[1] Burkett, Larry, *How to Manage Your Money*, Chicago, Moody Press, 1975, p.7.

God's truths, and the Lord used Larry to light a fire in Trevor's heart that still burns to this day.

The study wasn't simply about how to get out of debt, though this was certainly a topic that Larry often addressed. The first thing that Larry introduced in the study was the biblical definition of wealth. He quickly noted that "wealth is neither moral nor immoral." In other words, God never condemns wealth itself. There is no inherent virtue or condemnation in either wealth or poverty. "There are dishonest poor as well as rich," Larry noted. He concluded, "God condemns the misuse of or the preoccupation with wealth."[2] The second topic that Larry focused on was the concept of stewardship. This is the most important financial principle taught in Scripture, and I will focus on this in a later chapter.

Larry also discussed the "perils of money" and how many of us end up in "financial bondage" due to our improper (unbiblical) attitudes towards wealth. He wisely pointed out that a person can be in bondage through an abundance of money, or a lack of it. The type of bondage Larry described is anything that interferes with our relationships with our friends and family, and especially anything that interferes with our relationship with God.[3] Proverbs 22:7 says, "The rich rule over the poor, and the borrower is servant to the lender." Some translations use the word "slave" instead of the word "servant." The word "slave" is a good term to

---

[2] Burkett, Larry, *How to Manage Your Money*, Chicago, Moody Press, 1975, page 13.

[3] Burkett, Larry, *How to Manage Your Money*, Chicago, Moody Press, 1975, page 25.

describe the financial bondage about which Larry was talking.

As Larry weaved his way in and out of the Scriptures to teach the biblical principles of finance, he touched on numerous practical matters as well. Among other things, and along with specific plans on how to get out of debt, he taught on giving, investing, taking care of the poor, and budgeting. Larry taught on many specific financial topics that are important to most anyone. We have relied on this wisdom throughout our marriage of nearly 16 years.

Trevor and I had joined a small Baptist church the week after our wedding. It was a good compromise between my very contemporary Vineyard church and his very traditional Southern Baptist church. The decision of what church to attend was a major one for our young marriage, and it is a great example of God working in our lives. Our new church had solid Bible teaching and contemporary worship music, which was a must for me. We developed some strong friendships during that time and were able to be accountable to other believers in our areas of weakness. We were members there for the first three years of our marriage, at which point we were asked to join the Gainesville Vineyard Christian Fellowship, where my dad was the pastor, to become the youth group leaders.

After we went through the *How to Manage Your Money* study in those first months of our marriage, we were so excited about God's principles of managing money that we approached our church leaders and asked if we could lead the study at church. They agreed, and we advertised the study to the church and community. We had a pretty good turnout that first session, and we went on to lead the study multiple times over the next several years. It was truly life-changing.

In addition to leading that study for adults several times, we led the *God's Way of Handling Money* teen study after we became youth group leaders. The teens really seemed to grasp the principles, and lives were changed for the better through their study of God's Word. I love what Isaiah says in chapter 55, verse 11, "So is my word that goes out from my mouth: it will not return to me empty, but will accomplish what I desire and achieve the purpose for which I sent it."

As part of my training at Christian Financial Concepts, I was able to take the course to become a volunteer budget counselor. I loved maintaining our own family budget, so I thought that I would be able to help other families work through their financial challenges by developing budgets and plans for debt reduction.

I helped several couples and singles work on their budgets in the years following. There's an interesting thing that often happens with people who request budget counseling assistance. They usually are in the midst of what they deem a financial crisis when they reach out for help. They meet with the counselor for the first time and expect him or her to provide an immediate solution to their problems. Instead, this initial meeting involves instructing the couple or person to keep a spending log for the next 30 days in order to get an accurate picture of their spending. They also should start working through a financial Bible study so they will understand and take to heart God's principles regarding their finances (resources can be found at Crown.org, Compass.org, and DaveRamsey.com). Without this step, there is usually no lasting change in how one handles money, because, as was so emphasized in our pre-marital counseling, only God can truly change someone. There might be some actual work done on developing the budget during the first session, but it will be far from functioning well by the time they leave.

What I found is that so many people want a quick fix when it comes to their finances. They fail to understand that it usually took years to get into the financial difficulty in which they find themselves, thus it likely will take longer than one budgeting session to get out of it. Sadly, many of the people with whom I met did not return for a second session. I've heard the same thing from other budget counselors I know. The counselees might have found some sort of resolution to their situation, or maybe they thought that the process was too difficult to pursue. At any rate, I wonder sometimes how things turned out for those people.

5

THE BUDGET

"For the Lord gives wisdom, and from his mouth come knowledge and understanding." (Proverbs 2:6)

When I met Trevor, he was living in a small, one-bedroom apartment in Gainesville. It was totally a man-pad—with blinds that were too short for the windows, huge posters leaning against the windows to cover the gaps, no curtains, no pictures on the walls, and there was *ugly* furniture. After our honeymoon, I happily moved my clothes and all of our wedding gifts into our little apartment, rolled up my sleeves, and went to work making it our home. I slowly began to make some changes to make it more inviting, which Trevor seemed to appreciate.

Trevor admitted that he wasn't so great with money, so he gladly turned the checkbook, the bills, and all other financial business over to me. Trevor often talks about the irony of this decision—given that he held an undergraduate degree in physics with a minor in mathematics along with two graduate degrees in mathematics education. In addition, he had been the treasurer for several years at the Baptist church he had attended all of his life. In other words, he was good with numbers and could manage the accounts of others well, but when it came to his own finances, he was ready for someone else to take over, which verified what Larry taught so clearly in *How to Manage Your Money*, the importance of our attitude toward wealth. When I took over his checking account, there were several recent charges from the overdraft protection that had been activated. That had to be remedied right away.

Once home from our honeymoon, I dove into the process of creating a budget and a plan for getting out of debt. First, we did some "plastic surgery" on our credit cards. We cut up all but one, and we vowed only to use it in cases of emergency when we *both* agreed there was an emergency. Our goal was to train ourselves how to use this type of credit and not to use it again until we were completely out of debt. I listed all six of our debts on a piece of paper, the balances that we owed, and the interest rate for each one. We decided that we would pay minimum payments on all of our debts to keep them current but would focus on paying off the one with the smallest balance first by paying extra toward the principal each month. Once that debt was retired, we would roll everything that we were paying on the first debt into the next smallest balance debt, thus "snowballing" the payments. By the time we were working on paying off the biggest debt, we should have a really large amount going to it each month to eliminate it quickly.

I developed our budget based only on Trevor's income. His paycheck, after tithe, would pay for our rent, utilities, rental insurance, car insurance, food, toiletries, clothing, gas, and the minimum payments on all of our debts. Any extra from his check would go toward the smallest debt. When we received my paychecks, we gave a tithe off the gross. Then we put the entire amount that was left toward the debt that we were working on eliminating at the time. This helped us to pay off the smallest debts—the student loan, the engagement ring, and then the credit card—in what seemed like no time, just a few months, really. And yes, I paid off my own engagement ring because of the way that we were "snowballing" our debts.

The next debt to go was Trevor's vehicle loan. When I met Trevor, he was driving a Saturn sedan that he had purchased brand new, a no-no, he now realizes. I also had a small sedan, the used Corolla I had just bought, and he figured that we would need a small pickup truck as a married couple more than we would need two sedans, so he sold his Saturn at a loss, negotiated a payoff for the deficit with his bank, and took out a loan for $5,500 to purchase a small used pickup truck.

Next to go was the loan for the land ($6,900). Since it was the next to last debt to go, we had a pretty sizeable chunk of money going toward it each month. It didn't take long for it to disappear. Last of all was my $9,000 car loan. By the time we were focused on paying off my car, we were making payments of close to $1,600 a month on the loan. It seemed to disappear like butter in a hot pan!

When all was said and done, we were able to pay off all of our debts within 13 months of our wedding. Praise the Lord! What an amazing feeling it was to be completely out of debt.

Freeing up enough disposable income to pay off

$25,000 of debt within just over a year on our average salaries wasn't easy. We made some pretty drastic decisions to save money. I had used a "car phone" before cell phones were very widely used when I was traveling around making home visits as a social worker, so we made the decision to pay the early termination fee and cancel the phone. We hardly ate out; we rarely bought clothes, and when we did, we shopped at a really cheap clothing store near our apartment or at a thrift store. We didn't take expensive trips. We were as frugal as frugal could be.

Being in a lot of debt was very stressful for me. It didn't bother Trevor so much because he was used to it, but I didn't like it. One night very early in our marriage when he came home late from an out-of-town track meet, Trevor told me that he had given one of the students $10 to buy something to eat. I was so upset! I shouldn't have been because Trevor had been generous to someone who needed a hand, but I had so carefully budgeted every penny that even losing $10 stressed me. I remember a sweet friend at CFC encouraging me to loosen up a little and stop being so intense regarding saving money. She rightly told me that I needed to enjoy life, even while we were in the process of eliminating our debts.

Here were the basics of our budget. Remember, these numbers are from the late 1990s. We took a "Monthly Income and Expenses" sheet from the *Financial Planning Workbook*. (You can print the worksheet for free from the Find Help section of Crown.org.) Trevor's gross income was listed at the top, then below it we subtracted 10 percent of his gross pay (our tithe to the church) and the amount that was withheld for taxes. What was left was our Net Spendable

Income. We figured out how much we were spending in each category. It took some time of adjustment to determine what worked for the discretionary categories, but many of the expenses were already set. Trevor's teacher retirement withholding of $175.32 (7.3 percent of NSI) was mandatory, so we didn't have a say in how much was withheld for that, and before we met, he had elected to contribute an additional $50 each month into an annuity (2.1 percent of NSI). Our housing expenses were 25.6 percent of NSI ($616.75), which included rent, renter's insurance, power bill, mailbox fee, phone bill, cable, and maintenance. We budgeted $160 per month initially for food, which was 6.6 percent of NSI. The automobile category consumed another 26 percent of our NSI, which included payments, gas, insurance, license/taxes, and maintenance. We spent 2.3 percent of NSI on life and medical insurance. Debts consumed 18.2 percent of NSI (credit card, student loan, land, and my engagement ring). Entertainment/Recreation accounted for 5.8 percent or $140/month total for eating out, activities, and vacation savings. We budgeted $30 a month, or 1.2 percent of NSI for clothing. Medical expenses also accounted for 1.2 percent. Finally, Miscellaneous expenses such as toiletries, laundry, allowance, lunches, newspaper subscription, gifts, educator organization membership, extra giving contributions, and miscellaneous expenses accounted for 13 percent of NSI, or $314.40.

If you counted more than 100 percent, so did I. Our first budget didn't balance because our basic expenses were more than Trevor was bringing home. Fortunately, we were budgeting only on Trevor's income, so we had my income to make up the shortfall until we could pay some things off and eliminate some payments, but it shows how tight things were because of all the debt payments that were a part of our lives at the time. Do you see why I was so stressed? I felt like we had shackles on our feet because our finances were completely tied to our creditors. Galatians 5:1 expresses the longing of my heart during the early months of our marriage: "It is for freedom that Christ has set us free. Stand firm, then, and do not let yourselves be burdened again by a yoke of slavery." How I longed to be free from the yoke of slavery that debt represented in our lives!

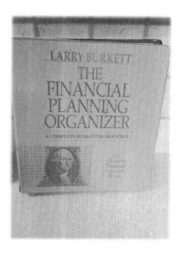

OUR BUDGET BOOK

What we learned is that a budget could help keep us from overspending in any particular pay period or in any particular area, help us plan for non-regular expenses (such as car repairs, vacations, or yearly insurance premiums), and help us plan for our financial future. A budget can play an essential role in helping to weather difficult financial times that many families have experienced over the last few years. The dramatic rise in gas prices and food prices in recent years have hit us pretty hard because of our family size and the large vehicles that we drive. We have had to adjust our budget down in many areas to accommodate the increase, especially in the gas category. Our budget is in almost constant flux, but having a budget helps us to see what adjustments we need to make in spending and therefore maintain sound financial discipline. Establishing a budget can be a lengthy process; it can take as long as a full year to get a budget working well, but the benefits are well worth the hard work that is involved.

A note here about credit cards: After we became debt free, we gradually began to use credit cards again, paying them off each month so that we never incurred any interest. Some financial teachers discourage the use of credit cards altogether, and I can see the merit in that advice, especially for those who struggle with misusing them. For us, it's a matter of convenience because we don't care to keep up with a lot of cash. To this day, we pay off whatever we charge each month, and we make sure that what we buy with the credit cards is covered in the budget. Some people choose to use debit cards instead of credit cards, which is fine, too. The thought of someone stealing my debit card and wiping out my checking account is a little scarier to me than someone stealing my credit card and making charges on it, though maybe that's a silly thought. Another reason I prefer the credit card to the debit card is that I have to make only one entry into the checkbook register each month when I pay off the card. With a debit card, each individual purchase must be recorded in my checkbook register. My time is pretty limited, so that step makes a difference, and it keeps me from possible mistakes in forgetting to record transactions.

Larry Burkett spoke to the use of credit cards many times. He often mentioned three basic rules for the use of credit cards that I think are very wise:

1. Use credit cards only for items that are in your budget. In other words, you have saved the money to pay for them.

2. Pay off your credit cards each month. Never pay interest on them.

3. If you ever find yourself in a position where you cannot pay off a credit card completely, destroy it and do not use credit cards again.

This is excellent advice for any generation. As Larry often pointed out, "credit is not the problem. It's the misuse of credit that is a problem." The draw of material things in this culture is strong, and the temptation to use credit to purchase those things is equally strong. We are an "instant" generation of live TV, microwave ovens, cell phones, FaceTime, and streaming movies online. We don't like to wait and save for items that we want. We tend to think that if we can fit a monthly payment for a desired item into our budget, then we can afford to buy the item. Before long, the payments add up, the interest builds, and we find that we're over-extended and we can't get our heads back above the water.

If we pay attention to what's going on in the federal government, we have a good example of how *not* to manage money wisely. This should not be surprising. Our government is simply a reflection of our culture. If the personal finances of a majority of the citizens of a democratic nation are a mess, then it is likely that the electorate will vote for politicians who share their financial values. The federal debt has grown to staggering levels in the last few years, and it's now at the point of being equal to the nation's Gross Domestic Product. That is dangerous and unsustainable. I often think that those in charge of the federal budget (not that they have even passed a budget for years now) should enlist the help of a panel of frugal housewives to show them how it's done. It's really a simple concept: spend less than you bring in, and save the rest for a rainy day.

6

THE CALL

"But seek first his kingdom and his righteousness, and all these things will be given to you as well." (Matthew 6:33)

While Trevor and I were in the process of paying off our debts, we were living in our little one-bedroom apartment and dreaming about owning a home. We knew that we wanted to have children one day, and I knew that I wanted to stay home to raise them, so somehow that drop in income had to fit into our future financial picture. As you might remember, a piece of land was one of the debts that we were paying off. Trevor bought the land with the intention of selling it to make a little money because he had gotten a pretty good deal on it. We listed the land for sale with a real estate agent, but it didn't move, so we felt that God was telling us that we should keep it and build a home on it someday.

During those months of paying off our debt, I used to make subtle comments to Trevor about our future home. I would say things like "God could provide a home for us without debt" or "Once our debt is paid off, we'll have a lot of money available each month to save to pay cash for our home. It won't take us *that* long to build a home with cash." We were living on such a shoestring budget that the vast majority of our income could be redirected toward saving for a home once our last debt was retired. Trevor thought I was insane. He had no intentions of building a home debt free, and he let me know that immediately. It *was* a ridiculous idea, I must admit. Who does that? We didn't know of anyone who had built a home with cash, at least not anyone on an average income like us. Maybe Trevor didn't want everyone to think we were out of our minds, or maybe he really didn't think that it was feasible.

Yet, I had a nudge in my spirit that wouldn't let up. I just had a feeling that God didn't want us to take out a mortgage to build our home. I was very uncomfortable with the thought of borrowing that much money, especially considering the stress that our relatively small consumer debt had caused me.

One thing I love about my husband is that he is open to hearing from the Lord, and when he does hear His voice, he obeys. He wastes no time in bringing about whatever it is the Lord has told him to do. About a year into our marriage, we were at church one Sunday morning worshipping the Lord with our church family. The service was nearing the end, and the music was playing. The congregation was standing, and Trevor turned to me and said, "Are you ready to make a commitment to the Lord never to borrow money again, for anything"? Without hesitation, I said, "Yes!" In his spirit, God had spoken to Trevor with that "still small voice" and revealed that He wanted us to commit never to take on debt again.

Trevor excitedly took me by the hand and led me to the front of our church. He asked the pastor if he could say something to everyone. Then Trevor told the congregation about the calling that the Lord had just placed on our lives. He said that he wanted our church body to pray for us, to keep us accountable, and to encourage us on our journey. We then left church and went to tell our parents about this calling, for we would need their help and encouragement along the way.

Looking back on it now, there wasn't much fanfare when we told our friends and loved ones about what the Lord had asked us to do. In fact, I'm sure that some people probably thought we were crazy. At that point, there was nothing really for others to get excited about; we were a young married couple still paying off debt and renting an apartment. We had little in the way of financial accomplishments. Almost everyone that we told about our "calling" was in debt at the time or had borrowed money for a home, cars, or credit cards, so our news might've even come across as a bit annoying.

Once we made the commitment to the Lord to remain debt free for the rest of our lives, we began to brainstorm how we could accomplish owning a home in a reasonable amount of time. The biological clock was ticking, and we knew that we wanted to have several children in the future. At that point, I was 25 and Trevor was 29, and we knew that we had to wait on children until we were in our home because I needed to be able to work full time to help pay for it. We had agreed that once we had children, I would stay home with them, so our income would be drastically reduced. Thankfully, I would soon receive a couple of promotions and pay increases at CFC, which would help a lot.

The rent at our apartment was pretty reasonable— around $450 per month plus utilities—but we knew that if we could eliminate those expenses, we would be able to save toward our home a lot faster. We talked about living with relatives, but we quickly ruled out living with our parents. We loved them, but we didn't think that it was best for our young marriage to be under either of their roofs, if they would even allow us to move in.

When I was finishing my bachelor's degree at North Georgia College several years prior to this, I had lived with my paternal grandparents in Cleveland during the weekdays and had gone home on the weekends. They lived about half the distance from the college than my parents did, so that living arrangement saved me a significant amount of time and gas. It was really an ideal situation. They were gracious hosts. I had plenty of quiet time to study, and I enjoyed spending that special time with them.

As Trevor and I were discussing ideas about ways to reduce our living expenses, I suggested moving in with Granny and Pa. We approached them with our thoughts, and they welcomed us with open arms. When Trevor's school year finished that May, we started packing up to move into the 400 square feet upstairs of my grandparents' home.

GRANNY AND PA IN 2013

One little aside here: Because Trevor is a teacher, he was off for the summer when we were preparing to move out of our apartment and into my grandparents' house. I would come home from work each day, and we would pack boxes together. Saying that he was just making my life more exciting, Trevor liked to hide from me when I would come home from work and then jump out and scare me. One particular day when I came home, as I walked by a rather large box in the center of the living room, Trevor jumped out of it and screamed. I nearly came out of my skin! I'm not sure why, but when I'm frightened I get angry. I was holding a prescription bottle in my hand when Trevor scared me, and before I could think about it, I flung it at him. I think that might have been the last time that my dear husband pulled such a stunt.

It took several trips in our little pickup to move all of our things to Granny and Pa's house. We had too much furniture to fit in the upstairs space since some furniture was already there, so we stored several things at our parents' homes. We settled into our new little home and went about the work of saving to build our house.

When we moved in with Granny and Pa, we were able to begin saving around $3,000 each month toward our house. We wondered how much we would need to save before breaking ground because once the process is started, a lot of money is required in a relatively short amount of time. We figured that $40,000 would be enough to begin breaking ground. That way, we could get close to "drying in" the house with the money that we had, and then we could slow the pace and finish the inside as we earned the money. Drying in a house means that the roof is on, the siding is finished, and the windows and doors are in. The house basically is weather proof at that point. For the next year or so, we worked, saved, dreamed, and planned for our home.

Besides saving rent money and spending time with my sweet grandparents, there was an added benefit of living with Granny and Pa. They have gardened all of their lives, preserving their extra harvest by canning and freezing the fruits and vegetables. My grandfather even ran a canning plant in their town for years while he was the agriculture teacher at the local high school. (He later served as the county School Superintendent and then went on to work for the Georgia Department of Education.) So, while

Trevor and I were living with them, Granny and Pa taught me a lot about canning veggies and soups, making jelly, and making creamed corn to freeze for the winter. When we moved out of their house, we left with many boxes of home-canned goods and a valuable education about growing and preserving foods.

7

SURVEYING

"We work hard with our own hands." (1 Corinthians 4:12)

After we had been living with Granny and Pa for about a year and as the next school year was nearing its end, Trevor began to feel the Lord leading him out of teaching, at least for a time. He wasn't sure what profession the Lord had for him next, but he felt that it was time to leave the public high school where he had been teaching mathematics for the past seven years.

Some people might think it foolish, but one benefit of this move, which we really weren't thinking about at the time, was that it allowed us to withdraw the retirement money that Trevor had saved during his teaching career and use it toward our house (around $11,000). This would help tremendously with our building costs. My grandfather cautioned us about withdrawing Trevor's teacher retirement money, but we felt that God had provided that money for us "for such a time as this," so we filled out the appropriate forms and cashed out the retirement account, adding that money to our building fund and getting closer to our goal of a debt-free home. At that point, we weren't very concerned about a retirement that was decades away, although we certainly understood the importance of putting money away for our future. Our focus was building the home as quickly as possible. Since we had committed to living debt free, and of course, that meant having no mortgage, we figured that we would be able to put extra away for retirement when we had finished our home, replacing what we had withdrawn, and adding to that. This has turned out to be the case.

Trevor had a friend who owned a land-surveying business. Trevor's dad had retired as a surveyor from the Georgia Department of Transportation some years prior, so Trevor talked to his friend about working for him as a surveyor. His friend agreed to hire him. Because Trevor would continue to receive his teacher pay through the summer months, though, he decided to wait a couple of months to start his surveying job so that he could work full time building our house.

Surveying was an interesting experience. Trevor started out making $7.50 an hour, and because it was a small business, he didn't get any vacation or sick time off or insurance or benefits of any kind. He worked long days, often in either the blazing Georgia heat or the bitter cold. Because he often worked in thick underbrush, occasionally he would come home covered in bug bites. A couple of months into the job, he received a raise: he was bumped up to $8 an hour. This was a humbling time in our marriage for Trevor. I was actually making more money than he was, even though he was working much harder and doing a great job at it. However, even with his meager pay, we still were able to budget all of our necessary expenses on Trevor's paycheck and use all of my income toward saving for the house. Also, this experience away from the classroom and in the world of small business was refreshing and informative for Trevor. His employers were strong Christian men who were committed to doing things the right way, and he learned much from them. Yet, we knew that we couldn't support a family on what Trevor was bringing home, and we didn't feel that he was using the gifts and the education that God had given him to his full potential in that job either. He felt the call back to education, but this time in a different environment.

We were nearing the end of 2000. Trevor checked the classified ads, and he happened to see that Riverside Military Academy, an all-boys school in Gainesville, had an opening for a math teacher. He sent in his résumé and was quickly called for an interview. The interview went great, and Trevor was offered the job. He drove over to my office and told me the news. He was offered $48,500 to teach mathematics, and the benefits were excellent. We were so excited and thankful for the Lord's provision. He began teaching at Riverside in January 2001 and was very glad to be the main breadwinner again. I must say that he looked quite nice in the army uniform that he wore at Riverside!

Trevor gained valuable experience during his six months of being a land surveyor. He enjoyed the friendships that he made, and he learned skills that he might never have gained except that he stepped out in faith to try something new. As I look back on that experience, I'm proud of my husband for many things: He didn't see himself as "too good" to work in a job that was really an entry-level position, and one that didn't require the degrees that he held; he worked hard and honored the Lord, in spite of the meager pay and long, hard hours; and he heard the Lord's call to go back to teaching when the right time came.

Because the military academy is a private school, Trevor paid into a 403(b) account for retirement. The money that he accumulated there would prove quite useful several years later.

8

FROM THE GROUND UP

"Wisdom has built her house; she has hewn out its seven pillars." (Proverbs 9:1)

OUR TORN AND TATTERED HOUSE PLANS.

During the first year of living with Granny and Pa (we lived with them a total of 26 months), while working and saving up for our home, we had made several trips to the local building supply store and looked through house plan books, dreaming of the home that we would one day build. We knew that we wanted several children, so we needed a house big enough for a large family. We were told that it would be cheaper to build "up" rather than "out," so we thought that a two-story home would work best. This was especially true for us because we knew that we would have to make some accommodations for our sloped lot. It's no wonder that Trevor got it so cheaply, because it really wasn't an ideal lot on which to build a home. For us, it would be best to have a smaller footprint and then build up as much space as we needed. We finally bought a plan book full of two-story house plans, and in that book we found a plan that we both loved, a two-story farmhouse style house with a large front porch. We studied the plan and dreamed of building it one day. We were told that we would need several sets of the blueprints during the building process, so our first large home building expense—around $550—was purchasing several sets of blueprints.

In addition to my full-time job at Christian Financial Concepts, I was in charge of all of the contracting for our house project. I made all of the phone calls to arrange for sub-contractors to come out and give us quotes; I made trips to the county planning and zoning office to obtain permits; I picked up supplies at various building supply stores; and I paid all of our construction accounts. One wouldn't realize without having built one's own home what a large job this is. I spent almost every lunch hour on the phone arranging details of our construction or running errands for it. It's no wonder contractors charge so much.

Larry Burkett used to say that a couple should not attempt to build a home until they have been married for at least 10 years because it's such an emotional and stressful undertaking. We started our home after about two and a half years of marriage, and was Larry right! Virtually every waking moment during this time was filled with "house stuff." Decisions and disagreements and frustrations and setbacks were all par for the course. A strong marriage was a necessity, and God was faithful. Thankfully, we didn't have children at the time; I can only imagine how much harder it would've been to include kids in the mix! Some people do it, though, and my admiration goes out to them.

Bob, a friend from our church, owned a swimming pool business, so he was experienced in earth moving, along with having the equipment to do it. We asked him for advice about grading our land. Our lot slopes downhill from the road, and it was just forest land at the time, so many trees had to be pushed down, and a level spot had to be cut into the side of the hill to make a place for our foundation. Bob came out to look at our lot with us and give us his thoughts. The house plan that we had chosen didn't include a basement, but because of the slope of our land, Bob suggested that we add a basement. He said that it would be an economical way to add more space to our house, and the slope of the lot was conducive to having a basement, so we took his advice. He then graciously offered to grade our lot for us, and he was so generous, charging us only $300 for the work that he did, pretty much doing it at cost. What a blessing—and we would discover that it was the first of many such blessings!

Adding a basement to our plan changed everything. We were told that it would be relatively cheap to finish our basement. Our plan became this: Frame the entire house (basement and two upper floors) and dry it in, then work on finishing the basement so we could move into it first. Afterward, we could take our time finishing the top two floors as we could afford it. Thankfully, our subdivision had very few covenants, so we weren't required to complete our building process within a certain time frame. Also, we were able to extend our building permit from the county year to year as long as we needed, so we weren't rushed in the building process by either of those sources. However, we didn't want our home to be an eyesore to the neighborhood for too long; therefore we worked hard to make sure it looked complete on the outside as quickly as possible. We have gracious neighbors who didn't complain, at least to us, about the length of time our construction took.

We drew out the basement plans ourselves. The footprint of our house plan was 1,500 square feet. That's the amount of area that we would have available on the basement level. However, because of the slope of our lot, we would need to move the garage to the basement level as well. We figured that we would make the garage about 22'x20,' which we have since discovered is a tight squeeze for large vehicles. We used about 70 square feet for the stairwell up to the main level (with storage underneath), and that left a little under 1,000 square feet for the basement living area. Taking that amount of space into consideration, we drew plans for a kitchen, living room, bedroom, bathroom, and laundry room—basically an in-law suite—on the basement level. This would be our living quarters until we could complete our top two floors, and we had no idea how long that would be.

OUR HAND-DRAWN BASEMENT PLANS.   **OUR BUILDING PERMIT.**

Near the end of 1999, we had our land surveyed ($330), submitted our house plans to the county for approval, paid the permit fees ($460), and obtained our building permit from our county planning and zoning office. We found out the requirements for building at our intended slow pace, and in December of 1999 we posted our permit on a tree on our lot, ready to get started.

Our land is a couple of lots away from Lake Lanier, and the county is diligent to ensure that construction projects don't result in sediment runoff into the lake. We were required to put up silt fencing before beginning our grading to keep mud from running down our land and into the lake. In February 2000 Trevor and I bought several rolls of silt fence, drove the stakes into the ground all around the back and sides of our lot to catch the runoff, and we were ready to break ground. Bob, our swimming pool friend from church, had one of his employees knock down trees with a bulldozer and grade a spot for our house. Over a couple of days, he cut a large level spot into the side of the hill and piled the trees below the cleared spot.

MICHELLE CLEARING BRUSH AFTER THE GRADING.

Thus began our part-time job. Every day after work, Trevor and I would go to our land to work on clearing the trees. For many weeks, we sawed the trees, dragged limbs into piles for burning, and stacked logs to be used later for firewood. A few times we paid some friends and family members to help us with this process, but most of it we did ourselves. Most people would have had their graders haul off their trees for them, but that was one expense we figured we could forego by doing the clearing ourselves. We had a few months to do it, too, because we weren't planning to begin framing until June when Trevor was out of school.

After the land was graded in February, we had several loads of dirt hauled in by a grader to make a driveway. For $6,200, we contracted with a company to pour our basement walls and a retaining wall to the side of the house. They came in, dug, and formed the footings to get ready to pour the walls. In the meantime, we hired a well company to drill our well ($2,400) because we don't have access to public water where we live. The well company drilled a 300-foot-deep, 6-inch diameter hole near the road at the top of our lot until they got the water pressure that they wanted.

OUR DRILLED WELL—300 FEET DEEP.

When a well is drilled, a lot of sediment runoff is produced. Unfortunately, the well guys weren't careful about where the sediment was going, and they let it run down over the bank into the cleared part of our land, filling up the forms for our basement walls. We were so very discouraged, but it was the first of a number of disappointing setbacks. The walls were scheduled to be poured within the next day or two, so we quickly had to shovel out all of that sediment before the concrete could be poured for the walls.

THE RUNOFF SEDIMENT FROM THE WELL FILLING THE FORMS FOR THE BASEMENT WALLS.

Soon, the basement walls and retaining wall were completed successfully, and we were excited to have an actual beginning to the shell of the house. To waterproof the poured walls, Trevor and I painted on a black tar-like substance all over the outsides of the walls. Then, the graders came to back-fill the dirt against the house.

Before the foundation could be poured, we had to have a plumber run drain lines under the ground that would take waste out of the house and into the septic tank. Hoyt, the grandfather of Trevor's brother-in-law, was a retired plumber. With the help of Trevor's dad, Hoyt did all of our plumbing under the slab, installed the well pump, and ran the water line from the well into the house to give us running water. We paid for all of the materials, of course, but Hoyt didn't charge us a cent for any of his labor. That was yet another huge blessing!

MICHELLE DIGGING FOOTINGS FOR THE SLAB.

Trevor and I then went to work digging the footings for our slab. We dug until our bodies ached, making trenches around the outside of our foundation to be filled with concrete, which would help to support the weight of our house.

GRAVEL WAS DUMPED INTO THE FOOTINGS THAT WE HAD DUG FOR THE SLAB.

We ordered a dump truck full of gravel that we had to

spread out over the foundation before we poured it with con-crete. If you can believe it, the truck dumped the gravel right into the footings that we had just dug. Not everything went our way, by any means.

We had to have the county inspectors come out to check the plumbing under the slab as well as the footings we had dug before we could pour the foundation. Because the back portion of our homesite was on a little bit of fill dirt, we were required to have a compaction test to make sure that the ground was packed enough not to settle from the weight of our house. We passed the compaction test and the plumbing and footing inspections, so we were ready to pour the foun-dation.

Because we wanted our home literally to be founded upon God's Word, just before the concrete was poured for our foundation (at a cost of $1,600), we buried a Bible under the ground in the corner of the house. After the house was framed, over several months' time, we wrote Scriptures all over the studs and above the door frames and on the boards inside the house. Some of our good friends from church, Ja-son, (a second) Jason, and Gary came over to help us with this task. We know that there is power in God's Word, and though these gestures were somewhat symbolic, we believe that our home will forever be rooted and founded upon the Lord.

TREVOR AND 82-YEAR-OLD UNCLE CHARLIE FRAMING THE HOUSE.

When school was out in June 2000, we were ready to begin framing the house. Our framers consisted of Trevor, Trevor's uncle Ernest, who was in charge of the framing, Trevor's dad Edsel, Trevor's great-uncle Charlie (82 at the time), Trevor's brother-in-law Chris, and Brad, the son of my friend Kim. What a crew!

We paid Ernest $15 an hour because he was in charge of the framing. We paid Uncle Charlie and Brad $10 an hour, and Trevor's dad wouldn't take any money from us during the majority of the building process. He helped with many, many different steps, which I'll discuss in more detail later, but suffice it to say that he saved us many thousands of dollars. We also didn't pay brother-in-law Chris because Trevor had helped build his house a couple of summers before.

I ordered all of the lumber and materials that we would need to get started, and we had it delivered prior to the day we would begin framing. This was the first of many loads of lumber. All told, the lumber, silt fence, house wrap, water-proofing supplies for the poured walls, additional grading and loads of fill dirt, labor, windows/doors, gravel, and miscellaneous supplies were over $30,000.

EARLY IN THE CONSTRUCTION PROCESS.

The framing phase of house construction doesn't take long, just a few weeks. The slow part is finishing the inside of the house. It's important to frame a house, get a roof on, and install windows and doors as quickly as possible to prevent water damage to the wood on the inside ("dry it in"). The framing crew had worked only one day when Trevor's grandmother, Edsel and Ernest's mother, got sick. She was taken to the hospital and passed away a few days later. Since two of her sons and her grandson were working on our house, the construction was suspended for about a week. Once they started again though, it was amazing to see how quickly the shell of the house went up. I went after work each day to help pick up scraps of wood, sweep up sawdust, plant grass seed, and complete any other chores that needed to be done. It was thrilling to see the changes taking place each day!

GETTING READY FOR SHINGLES. TREVOR'S DAD IS STANDING ON THE ROOF.

ROOF IS COMPLETED, AND WINDOWS AND DOORS ARE IN!

9

FROM THE GROUND UP— PART 2

"All hard work brings a profit, but mere talk leads only to poverty." (Proverbs 14:23)

We wrapped up the framing phase of the house construction within a few weeks. We paid somewhere around $25,000 for the lumber for framing, treated lumber for the porches, and some of the trim. We paid approximately $4,500 in labor costs to our family members and friends who helped us get the foundation ready and to do the framing. Trevor and his uncles built the roof and nailed down the tar paper, but they didn't feel comfortable doing the shingles, so we got a couple of quotes from roofers, bought the materials, and paid a sub-contractor to put on the shingles ($1,672 for labor). Within no time, we had a roof on our house and were ready for windows and doors. Trevor and his dad installed the windows ($1,890) and exterior doors ($1,336), and by this time it was really looking like a house.

SEE THE "HOUSE WRAP" ABOVE. TREVOR IS HANGING VINYL SIDING ON TOP OF THE WRAP.

Before installing siding, we were advised to wrap the outside of the house in "house wrap" to help keep out the elements and to help with insulation. We got a couple of staple guns and went to work wrapping the house with the big rolls of heavy-duty plastic wrap. This was quite a job in itself because some parts of the house are a *long* way from the ground. We got used to being on tall ladders or scaffolding over and over in those days. My younger brother Jeremy came a couple of times to help us with this big chore, for which we were very grateful. An extra set of hands at this time made things much safer.

Because of monetary constraints and because we wanted little long-term maintenance, we decided to go with vinyl siding for the outside of the house instead of brick or fiber cement siding. We agreed early on to have white siding with black shutters, for we really liked the traditional look. We got a couple of quotes from siding contractors, but to hire someone was going to cost a lot more than we wanted to put into it—between $9,000 and $12,000. So, we decided to hang the siding ourselves. We paid about $3,300 for the materials and a few hundred dollars more in labor for our friend Aron to help us with the difficult parts. Don, another friend from church with building experience, came over one day and showed us how to get started. Then from there, we started a months-long process of hanging siding most every day after work and all day on Saturdays.

SIDING ON THE CHIMNEY SIDE OF THE HOUSE.

We worked through the cold weather months when it would get dark shortly after we would get off of work and arrive at the house. Our sweet next door neighbors, the Keys, would sometimes set up a spotlight for us so we could see to work. They were so kind and encouraging to us during that time, and they have continued to be wonderful neighbors to us through the years.

Our friend Aron was skilled in many areas of construction. Along with siding, he did metal work and gutters. He helped us by doing the metal work along the fascia boards and installed our gutters, shutters, and chimney cap for us. We paid him $15 an hour for his help, in addition to the materials, and his assistance was invaluable to us.

We had used up basically all of our money during the framing phase, so taking several months to finish the siding on the outside of the house wasn't an issue. That gave us some time to save toward finishing the basement. The slowest part of finishing a house is the inside, but it's also the most expensive part. By the time we finished with the siding, we had saved some more money and could continue to finish the basement apartment.

Around this time, my uncle Mike had sold his farm and was not working full time. Instead, he was studying to receive a commercial pilot's license. He was very skilled in electrical wiring, and he offered to wire our house for us. My grandfather Pa helped him with it, so over the next several weeks the two of them patiently bored holes, pulled wires, and arranged all of the electrical circuits in our house. We paid for all of the wiring materials, but my uncle would accept very little in the form of pay for his services. We ended up paying him only a few hundred dollars for all of his help, and Pa would accept no pay from us at all. What a blessing!

Trevor's dad is skilled in so many areas; he ran all of the water lines throughout the house, in addition to framing, hanging windows and doors, and installing hardwood floors. Years later, we paid him to do some trim work and help build decks, but the majority of his labor was done at no charge. I can only imagine how much money he saved us. We hired a local plumber to run all of the drain lines for the house, but his fees were very reasonable—a total of around $1,000 for the labor. In case you were wondering, water lines are small PVC pipes that take water from the water holding tank or whatever your water source is to the faucets, toilets, dishwasher, and washing machine; drain lines are larger PVC pipes that carry waste out of your house into the septic tank or sewer system. Running water lines and drain lines takes different skills and knowledge, and Trevor's dad only felt comfortable tackling the water line part of the plumbing.

We had decided early on that we would go total electric for the house, and our power company, Jackson Electric Membership Corporation, had a program called Comfort Homes available at that time. It involved paying a company to come out during the construction of the home (after all of the plumbing and wiring was done, but before drywall was hung), to spray expanding insulation into all of the cracks and crevices of the home, around all of the windows and doors, and in every space that they saw. Basically, they made the home as airtight as possible, which helps tremendously with keeping our power bills down. After our construction was completed, Jackson EMC reimbursed us around $1,120 for the sealing services that we had purchased, and we have qualified for their lowest residential power rate—not a bad deal at all.

Before we could finish the basement, we had to hire a heating and air company to install all of the ductwork for the main level of the house because that ductwork had to go into the ceiling of the basement. It wouldn't be feasible to go back later to install that once the basement was finished. We wouldn't actually purchase and install the heat pumps for the top two floors until we were closer to finishing those floors, but the HVAC company went ahead and did the ductwork for the entire house and installed the air handler units up front. They also installed a through-the-wall heating/air conditioning unit, which still works great to this day, in the basement living room to heat and cool the entire basement apartment. We paid the HVAC company 60 percent of their total charge for the initial work ($5,355) and then the remaining 40 percent ($3,570) when they came back to bring the units and get everything running. The septic tank and fill lines were also installed around this time at a cost of $3,250.

Even though we got a lot of good advice along the way about constructing a home, and even though we experienced many blessings along the way, our efforts were not without some significant difficulties. Of course, this is going to be the case with most anything worthwhile. In addition to the forms being filled with runoff from the well and the footings being filled with a load of gravel, let me give you a couple of other examples. One happened as we were having loads of gravel brought in for the driveway, which was very early in the construction process, before we had really done anything to the foundation of the house. The lower side of our driveway slopes down at a pretty steep grade and it's mostly fill dirt. Unfortunately, the dump truck that delivered our gravel went off the steep downhill side of the driveway. The driver was able to back his truck in fully loaded and dump the gravel, but he was unable to pull the truck out empty. We were at work at the time, so we didn't find out about it until we got there that evening. The gravel company brought in a gigantic wrecker to pull the dump truck out. I'm sad to say that in the process, a big piece of the asphalt above our driveway was torn up. We learned that some of the neighbors down the road had worked long and hard just a few years prior to get the road paved, and they were none too happy to see a big hole torn into it.

ROAD DAMAGE ABOVE OUR DRIVEWAY FROM PULLING OUT A DUMP TRUCK THAT GOT STUCK.

We felt terrible. We wrote a letter to our neighbors apologizing for the mishap. We made a copy of the letter for each house on our road, a really short, dead-end street with only about eight other houses, and bought little gift certificate tokens to the local Dairy Queen for everyone. We delivered them to all of the houses, praying that they would forgive us; we really wanted to be good neighbors during our very extended building process and not cause trouble. The gravel company sent out a crew the next day and put a big asphalt patch on the damaged spot, but some of the neighbors still weren't satisfied. They thought the patch was temporary and that the section of road should be torn out and re-paved. It never happened, and the patch is still there to this day, though it is barely noticeable and functions fine. Thankfully time heals; the neighbors seem to have gotten over it, and we remain in their good graces.

We faced another trial a few months into construction. A man who originally owned our land (two owners before us) still lived on the street above us and came by occasionally to remind us that he used to own the land. He complained to the county planning and zoning office that our next door neighbors' house was too close to the road, but the planning and zoning office assigned the complaint to us because we were the only house still under construction. We received a notice from the county about the complaint that had been filed. We knew that we were close to the limit. The house was supposed to be at least 30 feet from the center line of the road, but our lot is so sloped that we had to put it as close to the front of the lot as possible to keep from building on too much fill dirt. The county came to measure where we were, and they said that our front porch was six feet too close to the road on one end and four feet too close on the other.

To keep from tearing off our front porch, we filed a variance with the county and went before the planning and zoning board to request that they allow us to keep our home where it was. We took pictures with us to show the board the challenge we faced with the slope behind the house, and we presented our case, praying that they would be merciful to us. They ruled in our favor, and our porch was allowed to stand. We had to pay a $200 fee to the county and go through the headache of the variance process, but again God showed us mercy in spite of our ignorance and inexperience.

MICHELLE PAINTING PRIMER ON THE BASEMENT WALLS.

Our main priority was getting the basement ready to

inhabit. We purchased insulation and installed it ourselves. Next, we hired a man to hang the drywall at a cost of $1,200. Drywall was another job that we didn't feel that we could do ourselves and make it look decent. We formed up and poured our driveway in the spring of 2001 at a cost of $2,178 for the concrete, plus labor for those who helped us. We hired our friend Aron to install our gutters and soffit at a cost of $1,251. We installed a bathtub, painted the walls ourselves with the help of my mom and dad, and then hired a company to hang the drop ceiling for $1,080. We purchased pre-made kitchen cabinets and countertops from a building supply store, and Trevor's uncle Benny, another brother of Trevor's dad, helped us install them at no charge. Just like Trevor's dad, Benny is skilled in many ways. He has a woodworking shop near his home where he has built everything from furniture to cabinets. Uncle Benny also cut and installed window sills for the three basement windows. We were very grateful and thankful for his help.

Trevor's Uncle Larry, another of his dad's brothers, works for a phone company. He volunteered to run our phone and cable lines, and he charged us nothing for all of his help. We then bought a toilet, a bathroom vanity, a water heater, a dishwasher, a washing machine, a clothes dryer, and a refrigerator from a building supply store. We bought a used range from a co-worker. Trevor's dad installed our toilet, bathroom faucets, tub fixtures, kitchen sink and faucet, and dishwasher. We contracted with a local flooring company to install carpet in the living room and bedroom and linoleum in the kitchen and bathroom at a cost of $1,525. We left the small laundry room floor concrete, as well as the closet off of the bedroom that contained the air handler unit for the main level of the house. My uncle installed our light fixtures and outlets in the basement. Whew! Finally, we were on the verge of being able to move in.

As you read all of the details about the people involved in building our house, were you struck by how many of our family members there were? We knew before we got started that we were blessed with many family members who could help us with construction, but looking back now, I'm simply amazed at the enormity of the outpouring of generosity that we received. It almost reminds me of an old-fashioned "barn raising," of course with the obvious differences being that we didn't build a barn and that we built over an extended period of time—not just a day or two. No, the Lord didn't drop cash in our laps because of our commitment to build debt free, but He surely provided in other miraculous ways!

By this point, it was mid-August 2001. We were ready for the inspection to receive the certificate of occupancy for only the basement. Although recounting the details makes the process sound like it took very little time, at this point, we had worked a year and a half to build a home and finish only the basement level sufficiently enough to move in. The county inspector was strict and rather emotionless. I suspect that it was out of the norm to request an occupancy permit when two full floors of the house were only studs, exposed wires, and plumbing, but when all was said and done, he granted us the provisional occupancy permit, and we couldn't wait to move in.

We moved only enough furniture into the basement to be able to sleep there on Thursday, August 23, 2001. We had to go out and buy a set of sheets because we had bought a queen-sized mattress set and had owned only full sheets up to that point. We fell into the bed that night exhausted but exhilarated because for the first time we were sleeping in *our* home.

When we knew that the time was close for us to be able to move into the basement about a month before we actually moved in, I asked Trevor about having a baby. His sister had just given birth to twin boys, and after holding those babies, my "mama" urge was going full blast. I was 27 and Trevor was 32, so the biological clock was speeding up. He agreed that we needed to start trying. As if moving into our own home wasn't enough of a blessing, we got up the morning after our first night there and had a very faint positive pregnancy test. Our first baby was on the way! Praise God, from whom all blessings flow!

Here are some pictures of the basement apartment:

THE BASEMENT LIVING ROOM, SHOWING THE THROUGH-THE-WALL
HEATING AND AIR UNIT MUCH LIKE THOSE IN HOTEL ROOMS.

THE BASEMENT KITCHEN LATER AFTER WE HAD CERAMIC
TILE INSTALLED ON THE FLOOR.

BASEMENT BEDROOM

10

FROM THE GROUND UP—PART 3

*"I praise you because I am fearfully and wonderfully
made; your works are wonderful, I know that full well."
(Psalm 139:14)*

Our baby was due early May 2002, so I had approximately nine more months once we moved into the basement to work full time and contribute toward finishing our house. Our plan was that I would stay home to raise and home-school our children, and we felt all along that we were going to have four babies. We knew that we wouldn't be able to finish the top two floors during my pregnancy and that our progress would slow down tremendously once our baby was born and I was no longer working, but we were content with that; it was time to expand our family.

During my pregnancy, we worked hard and finished what we could on the rest of the house. We had a large concrete retaining wall poured in the front yard ($5,257), garage doors installed ($1,290), and the fireplace and insulation installed ($3,900); we also did lots of smaller price tag items, but we still had a *long* way to go.

Spring of 2002 rolled around, and I was about to pop. Our baby boy was being stubborn and was in a frank breech position. At one point, the doctor gave me loopy drugs and tried to turn him around in my belly (called a "version"), but the baby was having no such thing; he was a big boy and was tucked inside me very tightly. We scheduled a C-section for April 24, 2002.

My last day working full time was bittersweet. As Larry Burkett's health had deteriorated, Christian Financial Concepts merged with Howard Dayton's Crown Ministries to become Crown Financial Ministries. I had made some lifelong friendships during my years there, and the Lord had used Larry and Howard and many others in my life in amazing ways. I had learned so much about what God has to say about finances, and it made a lasting, tangible difference in our lives. As I was packing up my things to vacate my cubicle the day before my C-section, I climbed up on a chair to retrieve something from an upper shelf. Howard Dayton happened to be walking by at the time, and I think I scared him to death. I'm sure the sight of a very pregnant woman standing on a chair was unsettling, though I really was fine. He quickly offered to help me and then carried my box of personal items to my car for me as I was leaving the office for the last time. Though I was sad that a very special chapter of my life was coming to a close, I was ecstatic about what was coming the next day!

CALEB'S CRIB IN THE BASEMENT KITCHEN.

Caleb Grant Thomas took his first breath at 12:15 P.M. on April 24, 2002, and our lives were forever altered, in an amazing way. I never knew I could love another human being the way that I loved that little creature. He was so helpless, yet so beautiful and so precious. Except for Caleb's fussiness and my getting almost no sleep, we were in heaven. We were cramped in our little basement apartment. The only place for Caleb's crib was in the kitchen. When it was time to put him to bed at night, I would lay him down in a portable crib in the bedroom so that we could stay up and watch TV for a while in the living room/kitchen area. Then when we were ready for bed, Trevor would carefully pick Caleb up and take him into the kitchen to his crib. This was a nightly routine for the year and a half that Caleb lived in the basement with us.

Near the end of my pregnancy, my boss at Crown had asked if I would be interested in working from home half time once the baby was born. I was in a leadership role in my department by that time, and I did a lot of editing responses that were going out to our constituents. I readily agreed to work half-time from home, for we desperately needed the income to be able to finish our house and move upstairs and out of the tiny basement apartment.

Five weeks after Caleb was born, I went back to work for Crown, but from home. I worked 20 hours each week, which was quite challenging to do while taking care of a fussy newborn. He didn't nap well for the first few months, so I had to grab work time when I could. I was nursing him, so sometimes I would let him go to sleep while nursing, and I would edit while he was asleep on the nursing pillow in my lap. It probably wasn't the ideal situation, but I did what I had to do to make it work. The income that I was able to bring in during that time was invaluable as we inched toward finishing the upstairs of the house.

Even now, years later, I work a tiny bit for Crown from home answering e-mails from people with financial questions, still thankful to be able to be involved in ministering to God's people in the area of finances. (You can learn more about the ministry on their website: crown.org. Chuck Bentley is their current CEO.)

In the months after Caleb was born, we had drywall installed upstairs ($7,500), painting done ($3,250), closet shelving hung ($376), fireplace mantle and marble installed ($800), and we purchased the hardwood flooring, ceramic tile for the kitchen, linoleum for the bathrooms ($2,385) and carpet for the bedrooms ($3,339). We contracted with someone to install the carpet and linoleum, but Trevor and his dad installed all of our hardwood floors. We put beautiful 3/4-inch cherry-stained oak hardwood in the foyer, living room, and dining room and a pretty natural oak color in the bonus room. It took several weeks for them to finish all of those floors, but with Trevor and his dad doing all the labor, we saved many hundreds of dollars. My sweet husband laid the ceramic tile in the upstairs kitchen, which took a long time to do. He had never done tile work before, so it was slow, tedious, and very labor intensive. He did a fabulous job with it, and his work stands to this day.

CUSTOM OAK CABINETS AND TREVOR'S TILE WORK.

For the kitchen, we ordered Corian® countertops ($2,158) and custom-made solid oak kitchen cabinets from Trevor's uncle, who was a cabinetmaker. We wanted them stained a dark cherry color to match our hardwood floors. He worked hard to achieve the look that we wanted, and they turned out beautifully. He also built long oak vanities for two of our bathrooms, two linen cabinets for the master bath, and two medicine cabinets in the matching oak. He did a fabulous job on all of the cabinets, and they still look great ($5,450).

As we talked and planned after that red letter day of the Lord's call on our lives to remain debt free, we often wondered if God might provide a large lump sum so that we could build our house quicker than relying solely on our wages and the slow process of saving and building as we went. We did commit never to go into debt again, so surely He would bless us in a really big way for being obedient to Him, right? Wrong. Even though we felt that we were obedient to Him all during the years of building our home, and though we did receive much, much help from our loved ones that equated to financial blessing, we never received any big financial gift or lump sum to help us complete the house faster. God provided for us in countless ways during that time, but we worked our fingers to the bone and no bags of cash ever fell from the sky.

It's important to note that our financial path was a specific calling for us, especially the way that we built our home. We certainly aren't saying that everyone's path should mirror ours exactly. We *are* saying that God and His Word are faithful and true and that He doesn't want His people burdened with enslaving debt. When God directs someone to do something, be sure that He will provide the means and the ability to accomplish it. In our case, He provided many talented family members and friends to help us build our home and steady jobs to pay for it. For others who might wish to build or purchase a home debt free or pay off a mortgage, God could provide in the form of an inheritance or significant pay increases or the gift of land or building materials or a myriad of other ways. God owns everything, so He can direct His resources however He chooses. The bottom line is that as we step out in faith and in obedience to do whatever the Lord has called each of us to do, He will *always* be faithful to see us through.

11

FILLING IT UP

"Sons are a heritage from the Lord, children a reward from him....Blessed is the man whose quiver is full of them." (Psalm 127:3,5)

We had to pay a fee to the county building inspector's office (I think it was $25) to renew our building permit once each year until we were completely finished with the house. We're grateful that our county allowed us to build slowly and didn't put a time limit on us as long as we kept our permit up to date. Also, we had to submit a letter at the beginning of each year to the tax commissioner's office to tell them what percentage of our house was complete. They based our property tax bill on that increasing percentage each year until we finally finished the house.

When Caleb was several months old, we began to yearn for another baby. I was unable to conceive while I was nursing him, so I weaned him on his first birthday. Two months later, in June of 2003, we found out that baby number two was on the way. We were very excited, but we knew that we had to finish the upstairs quickly. We just didn't see how we could fit two babies and ourselves in our little basement apartment, but by this time we were getting close to moving upstairs.

We finished installing the last of the plumbing and electrical fixtures, the interior doors, door knobs (I installed all of these), closet shelving, and so on. We scheduled one last inspection with the county, and we obtained our permanent occupancy permit and moved upstairs into the top two floors of our home in September 2003!

THE UPSTAIRS LIVING ROOM SHOWING THE HARDWOOD FLOOR.

We had finished the upstairs with the best materials that we could afford at the time. We splurged on some things, such as the custom oak cabinets, Corian® countertops, hardwood floors, and Berber carpet. However, we cut corners where we could, with the intention of going back later to upgrade and make things nicer. For instance, we installed linoleum in all of our main level and upstairs bathrooms initially, as well as the basement bathroom and kitchen. A few years later, we bought porcelain and ceramic tile and hired a contractor to tile all of those areas, as well as the landing areas at the bottom of the stairs beside the garage and inside the basement door ($2,820). Also, initially, we skimped on trim such as crown molding when we built, but a few years later we had additional trim installed and painted. When we chose our wall colors, I'm not sure what we were thinking. We used many bold and bright colors that were really more appropriate for a pre-school classroom than for a warm and inviting home. We ended up being pretty displeased with several of them, so we hired a painter a few years later to paint more neutral earth-tone type colors in several of our rooms. We live and learn.

We learned the hard way that it's not always a good idea to scrimp on some things. Here's a little advice for any of you who might be considering building a house: If you have small children or if you plan to have children in the future, please make sure you buy at least one toilet that is powerful enough to flush a dead squirrel. Now, we haven't needed to flush any dead rodents, but you would not believe it if I told you how many times our tiny children have stopped up our toilets with their bodily functions.

I suppose we scrimped on toilets. We just didn't realize we were scrimping at the time. We thought that spending hundreds of dollars on each toilet was useless when we could buy ones that looked nice for under $100 each. In other words, we went on appearances rather than function. We thought all household toilets functioned pretty much the same way. Since we have five toilets in our house, that was a lot of money for the toilets and seats. Boy, have we learned our lesson! Our kids stop up one or more of our toilets at least weekly, literally. We have plunged potties hundreds of times since we've had children. Trevor is quicker to plunge, but I prefer to take the slow approach and flush multiple times a day for several days until the toilets finally give in and flush.

Yes, we are super-frustrated with the low-water-use, government mandated toilets. If the government only knew how many thousands of gallons of water that we have wasted because of their water-conserving toilets, they might reconsider such regulation. But then again, probably not.

We have been tormented for about nine years now by our poorly flushing potties since our 11-year-old started stopping them up. Trevor has had it, and he said recently that he is going to invest in one toilet that will actually flush effectively. The kids all will have to use that one bathroom when they need to go, so sometimes they might have to wait in line, but hopefully a good toilet will save a lot of frustration down the road!

We have finished and upgraded and added a number of other things through the years as we could afford them: We had our two retaining walls and the side of the house bricked with Trevor's summer school income one summer ($5,105). With my part-time wages, we added a white vinyl fence, which Trevor installed along the driveway ($840); we added a ceramic tile backsplash in the kitchen, a couple of decks in the back yard (approximately $5,000) with Trevor and his dad doing most of the labor, a security system ($1,858), a cedar playground, lots of landscaping, again, by Trevor's efforts. Our landscaping has become one of his favorite hobbies. Each item has come gradually as we saved the money to pay for it.

Would it have been wonderful to have a completely finished house, trimmed with many extras, latest appliances and furnishings when we moved in? Absolutely! Would it have been worthwhile still to be paying on those items many years down the road? Not for us. The peace that we have from owing no one, owning outright everything that we have, far outweighs any desires that we have for the biggest and best things. We are content because we know that our Heavenly Father loves us and provides for our every need in His perfect timing.

Our second baby was born in March of 2004, another son, Jesse David. He was a sweet, pleasant baby and to this day is our compliant peacemaker. He is a joy to parent. Jesse and his older brother Caleb are extremely close. From the first day, we have instilled in Caleb and Jesse that they are and always will be best friends. They share everything together and love each other dearly. Jesse looks up to Caleb, and Caleb adores his Jesse. Each complements the other well. Caleb is very strong-willed and loves to lead. Jesse is very much a peacemaker and is eager to please. They have their squabbles, as do most siblings, but they always make up quickly and sincerely. We look forward to watching them grow to be lifelong friends.

Our only daughter Caroline Suzanne was born in February 2006. She is a feisty tomboy princess. She keeps up with her brothers in karate, Star Wars, and Legos, yet she enjoys shopping, new clothes, jewelry, and sometimes dressing up like a little lady. Caroline is a lot like Caleb in that she is very strong-willed and determined. Our house seems to be filled with such people, including Trevor and me! Though such traits can make parenting more difficult, such personalities can also serve them extremely well, especially as they grow into adults. From the moment Caroline was born, I felt that she was my kindred spirit. It's not that I love her any more than my boys, of course, but I have always felt that we share a special bond and that she understands me. She's my girl.

We found out in August 2007 that we were expecting baby number four. My due date was May 2008, which would give us babies born in February, March, April, and May, each not quite two years apart. We were thrilled to be expecting again, and I felt really good for the first few weeks, which was unusual for me. Most of my pregnancies had involved a lot of morning sickness during the first trimester. I should've known that something was wrong. During church on Sunday, September 23, just seven weeks into the pregnancy, I started bleeding. I was devastated. I had never had any such issues with my other pregnancies, and I knew in my spirit that we were losing our baby. I went to the doctor the next day, and the ultrasound showed the baby with no heartbeat. The ultrasound technician tried to assure me that it might just be too early to see the heart beating, but later that day I started contracting really hard, and the next morning I lost the baby.

I called Trevor at work to tell him what had happened, and he rushed home to us in tears. We lovingly placed our baby in a small box, went outside with our three young children, and buried our tiny baby in our flower garden in the front yard, asking God to comfort our hearts and heal us and knowing that one day we would be reunited with the precious little one who had just left my womb. It was interesting to see how God placed certain individuals in our path during this time to minister to us. Trevor had a coworker who had lost a child at a much later date during pregnancy, and just after leaving our doctor's office after we saw no heartbeat we ran into a church friend who was perfect to minister to us, especially Trevor.

This began the darkest time of my life. Even though I had three healthy, precious children, my heart ached for the one that I had lost and I longed for another baby to fill my womb. We had never had trouble conceiving up to this point, but a few months and several cycles passed with multiple negative pregnancy tests. Each month, I would grieve the loss of our little one all over again. It even made me cry to see pregnant women out in public. I felt like a crazy person. When I think about our loss even now, it still brings tears to my eyes.

In the Lord's mercy, we conceived again after what seemed like an eternity but was in reality only a few months. I gave birth to Noah Patrick in October 2008. Noah is a typical last child: full of joy and such a little ham. He was an absolutely yummy baby, so happy

SWEET CAROLINE FEEDING NOAH.

and an easygoing little fellow. Even though it still saddens me to think of the baby that we lost, I know that without that sorrow we wouldn't have had our precious Noah. I think of the Scripture in Psalm 30:5, "weeping may remain for a night, but rejoicing comes in the morning."

I wonder sometimes about God's purpose for taking our little one so early. I can only speculate until I'm able to ask Him face to face, but one thing I do know is that now I can sincerely relate to the anguish of miscarriage when a friend or acquaintance experiences it. I understand words that might bring comfort and words that will make the pain more severe, for I received both. I pray that in some way through my pain I can "carry [a dear sister's] burdens, and in this way [I] will fulfill the law of Christ" (Galatians 6:2). Isn't that

what God wants for us? He comforts us so that we can be a comfort to others? "Blessed are those who mourn, for they will be comforted" (Matthew 5:4). Thank you, Lord!

THE "NURSERY," WHICH IS THE SMALLEST BEDROOM ON THE TOP FLOOR.

Where did we put all of our little blessings? The top floor of our house has a nice big bonus room and three bedrooms, two small ones and the master. We made the smallest bedroom into the nursery, so first Jesse, then Caroline, and last Noah occupied that room. Each spent about two years in that room. The other small bedroom started out as Caleb's and then became Jesse's and then Caroline's as each subsequent baby was born. When Caroline was born, we moved Caleb into the bonus room and got a big boy race car bed for him.

However, he liked having Jesse in the room with him, so we put Jesse in a toddler bed in the bonus room with Caleb. Eventually, we got a bunk bed with a double on the bottom and a twin on top so Caleb and Jesse can sleep

THE BONUS ROOM/CALEB AND JESSE'S BEDROOM.

together. They love their room. Since it's the bonus room, it has cool sloped ceilings with five small doors going to storage behind the knee walls. It also has two dormers that looked like little empty hallways, so we put doors at the end of both and made them into closets for the boys' clothes. Their room is filled with Legos and action figures and posters and Webkinz and their special trinkets. Caleb and Jesse are best friends forever, and at this point they want to live

together for the rest of their lives. It warms my heart.

THE MASTER ON MAIN, WHICH IS THE PLAYROOM/OFFICE/GUEST BEDROOM RIGHT NOW.

The master bedroom is on the top floor also, along with a master bath. Because we had to put the garage on the basement level, what was to be the garage in the plans is now a large room on the main level that we use for a play room/office/guest bedroom. One day that room will probably become the master bedroom, but right now we feel more comfortable sleeping in the master bedroom on the same floor with our babies.

We're thankful for all of the space that the Lord has given us. Including our finished basement, our house is around 3,500 square feet, and we have been blessed at various times to share our home with others, as a way to "pay forward" all of the help and blessings that we received while we were building.

For instance, just a couple of months after we moved upstairs out of the basement apartment, my sister and her husband moved home to Georgia from New York. Mark had worked for Word of Life in upstate New York for several years, but they wanted to settle in Georgia, close to family. They knew that they wanted to build a home eventually, but they wanted to save up for a while so they wouldn't have to finance too much. We offered to let them live in our basement apartment, much like we had lived with Granny and Pa. They lived with us for a little over two years while they saved for their home.

It was a wonderful time when Suzanne and Mark were living with us. Suzanne hugged my babies almost every day. She had missed out on the first several months of Caleb's life because of living in New York, so she enjoyed making up for lost time. When Jesse was born, she was there to help me with the adjustment of having a newborn and a 22-month-old. She is an R.N. and she worked at that time in the Neonatal Intensive Care Unit at our local hospital, so she was well qualified to help me with my babies.

Suzanne and I would take turns cooking supper each night or sometimes both cooked parts of a meal, but we almost always ate together as a group. My children call my sister "Nana," a name that Caleb gave to her, and they have always been very close to her. Sometimes while Mark and Suzanne lived with us, Caleb would call down through the vent in our living room into the basement to ask "Nana" to come upstairs to see him.

Suzanne and Mark had their first baby while they were living in our basement, and just like my Caleb, their daughter Ashlyn had her crib in the basement kitchen. We loved being so near to each other's children for that short time. They moved out when Ashlyn was eight months old into a rental house near land that they had purchased for their home. Their house is in the county south of us, about 40 minutes from us, so we don't see each other as often as I would like, but I will always treasure the special memories of that time with my sister.

Suzanne and Mark had bought four acres of land, and the plan was that they would sell about half of it to Trevor and me so that we could build a home next to them. We had found out about the death of our great uncle, Robert Knight, former mayor of Coral Gables, Florida, and that we were listed as beneficiaries in his will. With our inheritance of $40,000, we had just enough left after our tithe to purchase one and a half acres from Mark and Suzanne for $35,000

THE BACK YARD WHEN IT WAS JUST GRASS.

plus closing costs.

We intended to build a home on the land, which is five minutes from my parents' house. We felt like we were not very near to anyone where we had built our house, and I, especially, longed to raise my children close to my sister and her children. When Caroline was two months old, in April 2006, we put our house on the market. This was just before the housing market crashed, so it was still very much a seller's market. Trying to sell a home with a newborn and two toddlers was absolute misery. I had to be ready at a few minutes' notice for showings, which is extremely difficult with three small children, one a nursing newborn, and because the market was so active at that time and we live in a very popular school district, the house showed over 50 times during that six-month listing period.

CURRENT VIEW OF THE BACK YARD FROM THE HOUSE.

Many of the people who saw our house loved it, and we were in the top two choices for several of them, but we never received a single offer. The slope of our lot was a big drawback, and people just couldn't get past that. The backyard was just a big sloped hill of lush green grass. Since then, we have added a lot of features to the backyard to make it much more useable: 40 cross-tie steps down the middle of the yard, which Trevor laboriously installed, lead to a large deck, a playground area, a fort for the kids, and about half of the grass has been replaced by landscaping with timbers, plants, and pine straw. I truly believe that if the backyard had been in the condition that it is now, it would have sold that summer. We listed the house for several subsequent six-month periods with various other real estate agents, but it showed only a handful of times because the market had tanked by that point.

VIEW OF THE BACK YARD FROM THE BOTTOM DECK NOW.

After seven years of teaching at the military academy, Trevor made the decision in 2008 to go back to the public school system. Trevor loved working at Riverside Military Academy and had many friends there. The decision to leave was almost exclusively financial, and as I alluded to in a previous chapter, having a formal written budget played a huge role in helping us make this decision. The military academy was suffering financially in the sluggish economy, which resulted in no pay increases for several years in a row. We had added several children, and we needed more income. Trevor went to a job fair in the spring of 2008 and was quickly hired by our county school system, which gave us an instant raise of around $12,000 annually. Praise the Lord! After Trevor had been back in the public schools for three years, he was eligible to buy back the seven years of service that we had cashed out to help with financing our home when he left Gainesville High School. We withdrew a little over $23,000 from his 403(b) that he had invested at the military academy and bought those seven years back. Then after a couple more years of teaching in public school, Trevor was eligible to purchase the seven years of private school time from the military academy at a cost of $127,000. Unfortunately, we didn't have enough left in the 403(b) to buy that many years, so we purchased three years of private school service for $40,333.

The school where Trevor now works is about 10 minutes from the land that we bought from Mark and Suzanne, for we had expected to sell our house and build a house there. However, God apparently had different plans, because our house never sold. Trevor has been commuting about 30 minutes each way to that same school for over five years now, while there is a high school in our system just a couple of miles from our house. He likes teaching where he is, but it just doesn't make sense to continue that commute if we're not going to build nearby. We're praying about asking if he can transfer to the high school that is close to our house, which likely would save us $1,500 to $2,000 in gas each year at today's gas prices. God is in control of that move, however, and we will trust Him to work it out in His timing, as He always does.

12

AUTOMOBILES

"Pride goes before destruction, a haughty spirit before a fall." (Proverbs 16:18)

Where we live in northern Georgia, there's no public or private transportation system. We're in a rural area, so having an automobile is a necessity for us. When we married, you might remember that I had a two-year-old Toyota Corolla and Trevor had a small Chevy pickup truck that was several years old. Those vehicles served us very well for many years, but as our family began to expand, our need for larger vehicles increased.

OUR MINIVAN THAT I REGRET SELLING.

After our second baby was born, we decided to invest in a minivan because we knew that we wanted two more children and we were running out of room in our small vehicles. We were somewhat ignorant about purchasing cars, and we were also fairly new to the Internet. We went online and found a really nice-looking, low-mileage, used Nissan Quest van at a dealership south of Atlanta. It had a "special online price" of around $16,000. We made the trip down to look at it, and it seemed like everything we wanted, including a VCR system to occupy the kids on long drives. We came home to talk and pray about it and decided that we would scrape together the money that we needed to buy it. We negotiated a drive-out price with the dealer for $16,000 cash.

Shortly after our third baby was born, we decided that Trevor needed a larger vehicle so that we would have two vehicles we all could ride in, in case we had trouble with one of them. We looked online for used Ford Expeditions and found one that was several years old but with relatively low mileage. We went to look at it and liked it, so we paid about $9,000 cash for it. In car decisions we always consult with my brother-in-law, Mark. He has made auto repair into a part-time business for himself and even built a garage, complete with a lift, adjacent to their home. He has given his stamp of approval on almost every auto purchase we've made.

Then, when we were pregnant with our last baby, in the spring of 2008, I got an itch for an Expedition, too. The mini-van was feeling cramped for four car seats, and Trevor's Expedition had so much more room in it. I'm afraid that maybe some pride had crept into my life in wanting to trade my van for an SUV, too, for which I'm ashamed. I allowed myself to get caught up in the excitement of a nicer, bigger vehicle, and I didn't allow the Lord to guide that decision. So again, we looked online and found a 2001 Eddie Bauer Expedition with low miles for sale. The owners were asking $10,500. I spent hours cleaning up the van and we advertised it around Trevor's school. Someone from school brought her mother-in-law to look at it, and we sold it to the mother-in-law for $7,000. We had only had the van for about three years, and we had paid $16,000 for it. I still regret the decision to sell it. I believe that selling the van after such a short time and taking the loss that we did was probably the worst financial decision we ever made. We used the $7,000 that we got for the van and took $3,000 from our savings to buy the Expedition for me for $10,000. It has been a good vehicle, too, for which I'm thankful, but it gets terrible gas mileage, though not a lot worse than the minivan.

Around the time we bought my Expedition, we sold Trevor's little Chevy pickup truck for $1,000 to buy a larger truck. We wanted something that we could ride in as a family, if necessary. He happened to be driving home one day and a neighbor on the street above us was selling a 1999 extended cab Dodge Ram truck for $2,850. Trevor snatched it up. It hasn't been the greatest vehicle in the world, but it has served us fairly well for what we've needed through the years. Trevor uses it to haul off our trash and recyclables to the county dumpster site every couple of weeks and to haul things for the house and yard: pine straw, hay, plants, lumber, or other odds and ends.

Our vehicles were made in 1999, 2000, and 2001, so they are fairly old. They are all running fine and we maintain them as best we can. I'm not sure when we will need to replace them, but I do know that God will provide when the time comes. He always has and He always will.

We talk occasionally about how nice it would be to have newer, better cars. We sometimes look online at newer vehicles and dream about what we would like to have if money weren't an issue, but that's dangerous for us. It tends to make us discontented with what we have, and it can lead to poor financial decisions, like when we sold our van. We're only human; we enjoy nice things. As Larry Burkett often pointed out (he had his weaknesses as well: old cars and tools), if you want to avoid spending money that you don't really have on things that you don't really need, then stay out of the stores, and just as appropriate today, off of the shopping websites. We are driving what we can afford, and we're thankful for the Lord's provision.

I like what Larry Burkett used to say often about cars, "Drive your car until it's dust, and then sweep up the dust and drive on the dust." Automobiles are not investments; they lose value almost constantly. They shouldn't be used as status symbols but as a means of getting from point A to point B safely and economically. It's almost never wise to purchase new vehicles. They lose much of their value the first time they are driven off of the lot. Buying a car that is a couple of years old, with low mileage and that even has some warranty left on it makes much more sense financially than purchasing a brand new car. My advice is this: Take your time and shop around. You will usually get a much better deal buying from a private seller than from a dealer. Just make sure to have the vehicle checked out thoroughly by a trusted mechanic. Most importantly, pray and seek the Lord's direction. A vehicle is important to many of us, and choosing wisely can benefit your pocketbook for many years.

13

HOMESCHOOLING

"Train a child in the way he should go, and when he is old he will not turn from it." (Proverbs 22:6)

I've always wanted to homeschool. Many years before I had children, before I even met my husband, I knew that I wanted to teach my future children myself. It's not that I had any homeschooling experience to draw from; I went to public schools all the way through college. Maybe that's why my desire to homeschool was so strong. I know what public schools can be like, and I wanted something different, something better for my family.

When I was in college, I volunteered at a crisis pregnancy center in a nearby town. I got to know two precious ladies who were in leadership positions at the center, and both homeschooled their children. I saw how much time they were able to spend with their kids, how close their relationships were with them, how respectful the kids were, how much the kids enjoyed being together. It inspired me. A seed was planted in my heart back then that the Lord grew and cultivated for many years until I had my own babies. It took some convincing to get Trevor to agree to the whole homeschooling idea. Of course, he's a public school teacher, so he assumed that our future children would go to public school.

Trevor wanted not only a strong education for our children, but also all of the extra opportunities such as sports and clubs that public schools typically offer. Homeschooling was a totally foreign idea to him, but the Lord (and I) worked on him, and little by little he came around to the idea of letting me teach our children at home. Early on, Trevor would say that maybe I could teach the kids through elementary school or for the first few years, and then they could go to public school or private if we had the opportunity, but as the years passed—given the many disadvantages of secular public school that he has witnessed first-hand—and as Trevor eventually saw the many benefits of homeschooling, he has become completely convinced that homeschooling is best for our family.

More and more Americans are opting for homeschooling. Since 1999, the number of American children who are homeschooled has grown by 75 percent. This growth rate is seven times faster than the growth rate seen in the public schools. Parents choose to homeschool for a myriad of reasons, but typically the choice to homeschool is rooted in a desire by parents to teach their children according to the morals and values of the parents and not those of the state. In addition, it is easier to vary styles of instruction, pacing, and level of rigor when in a homeschool environment. According to *USA Today*, "…homeschoolers, on average, scored 37 percentile points above public school students on standardized achievement tests."[4]

---

[4] http://usatoday30.usatoday.com/news/education/story/2012-02-14/home-schools-secular/53095020/1

In addition, according to one of the more recent studies on home education by Sandra Martin-Chang, Odette Gould, and Reanne Meuse, "structured" homeschooling (such as that provided by a homeschool academy) provided educational outcomes that were superior to public schooling in every measure. Children who received structured home-schooling scored better in all seven subtests. The subtests were Letter-Word, Comprehension, Word Attack, Science, Social Science, Humanities, and Calculation.[5]

My associate's degree is in early childhood education. I went on to earn a bachelor's degree in sociology, and obviously I didn't pursue a teaching career, but I always felt capable of educating my own children, nonetheless. Add to that Trevor's training and experience as a math teacher, along with an undergraduate science degree, and by the time our kids came along, we felt like we were as prepared as any couple could be to provide a great education for our children.

Those of us with children know that we don't just start teaching our kids when they turn five or begin kindergarten. Learning is a lifelong process. We teach them shapes, colors, and letters before they can even talk; we read to them; we converse with them in the car and show them how to use money at the grocery store; we teach them all about God's amazing world. Kids learn every day. When they hear us speak with correct grammar and sentence structure, they learn how to put language together correctly. When we let them "help" us cook, they learn to measure, to stir, to crack

---

[5] http://gaither.wordpress.com/2011/07/29/a-new-study-on-academic-achievement-of-homeschoolers/

eggs, and to count. When we sing to them (at least when I do, not Trevor—he will admit!), they learn pitch and rhythm and tempo. All of these early lessons form the foundation upon which higher instruction naturally builds. We want our kids to love learning.

With our first child Caleb, I purchased a traditional, workbook-based curriculum and in 2007 began teaching him at the kindergarten level when he was five. I was very ignorant about the plethora of homeschool resources that were available at that point, so I believe that the curriculum I chose was not the best one for his learning style or personality. However, he did well and we got through it. We tackled first grade the next year, which was interesting with three younger children underfoot. I would work with Caleb in the mornings while my youngest, Noah, napped, and I would have Jesse, who was four years old, help entertain Caroline, who was two years old. It worked, but it was getting more difficult.

The next fall, I added kindergarten to the mix for Jesse. The curriculum was a breeze for him; he is very much an auditory learner, and he had picked up *so* much from Caleb's instructional time. When I look back now, I wish I had started Jesse in first grade rather than kindergarten, but nonetheless, we finished the school year well. Jesse was such a compliant little thing that it was a joy to teach him.

The next fall got interesting. I agreed to keep Trevor's two-year-old niece during the week while her parents worked. At that point, I had Caleb in third grade, Jesse in first grade, Caroline was four, Noah was two, and Trevor's niece was two. Wow! I had my hands more than full. We needed the money that the childcare brought in, but that was one of the most difficult seasons of my life, trying to juggle all of those different children and their needs, managing a household, working from home part time, maintaining the books for our church, and keeping up with the day-to-day chores. Even though I was surrounded by kids all the time, I felt very lonely and isolated. I had no real friends that I talked to or got together with regularly, other than my sister, and we hardly saw each other. I had not really connected with any other homeschooling families because I had always had a napping baby in the mornings and afternoons and I wouldn't get out. Trevor will tell you that I'm a nap Nazi; my kids did not miss their naps. The trade-off was that we didn't get out and do much to make friends, not that it would have been very pleasant to take five kids under the age of nine out of the house, anyway. We trudged through those tough days that were not nearly as structured as I wished, and I tried to make the best of it for my kids, stressed though I was.

The next fall (2011), it was time for Caroline to start kindergarten. I bought the same workbook-based curriculum for her that I had been using for the boys. At first, she was excited and she did well, but gradually she began to complain and dislike what she was doing. So that I could manage teaching a fourth grader, a second grader, a kindergartener and care for two toddlers, I had decided to use a DVD curriculum with workbooks for Caroline. Basically, she watched a kindergarten classroom on DVD and was to participate along with the class as they learned and completed their pages. I know, it sounds really boring, right? It did *not* work for Caroline. She was much more interested in playing with Noah and with Trevor's niece, both three years old by this time, than she was in doing kindergarten work. I was having an increasingly difficult time managing the load.

By this time, we had started a wonderful piano class for Caroline. It consisted of a group of parents going through a six-year piano course along with their children. It was fun to get to know the other families and to learn piano along with our children. Caroline and I both were beginning to make some friends, so I was thankful. One of the moms in Caroline's piano class told me that they homeschooled, but they did it a little differently than most. She has four children also, but her older two children were enrolled in a Christian homeschool academy that met in a nearby church. They went to "school" three half-days each week, and the other two days she taught them at home. The academy was based on the Charlotte Mason philosophy of education. Charlotte Mason was a teacher in England in the 1800s who revolutionized the entire educational system of the day. She eventually began a school for teachers, and she taught future educators how to lay a "feast" of wonderful ideas before the children and encourage a love for learning. The Simply Charlotte Mason website defines the Charlotte Mason approach as "a method of education popular with homeschoolers in which children are taught as whole persons through a wide range of interesting living books, firsthand experiences, and good habits."[6] The children at the homeschool academy take na-

---

[6] SimplyCharlotteMason.com

ture walks, memorize Scripture, conduct science experiments, study artists and composers, and read "living" books, in addition to learning the basics of math and grammar. This arrangement gives the kids plenty of time with other Christian friends and another teacher and also plenty of time to learn at home. It sounded like the perfect solution—a Godsend—for our family.

I attended an open house for the homeschool academy in January 2012, and I fell in love with the school, the teachers, and the philosophy of education that I saw. The teachers emphasized cultivating a love for learning in the children— something that I don't feel that I had fostered very well in my kids to that point. However, I discovered that enrollment was almost full for the fall. I was in a panic. I didn't know what to do; I desperately wanted my three school-aged kids to be there in the fall. My piano class friend suggested that if I went ahead and enrolled one of my kids for the remainder of that school year, I would be ensured of having spots for my other two kids that fall. Immediately, I *knew* which child would be attending the rest of that year—my little social butterfly Caroline.

**FIRST DAY AT THE HOMESCHOOL
ACADEMY 2012.**

In early February 2012 Caroline started attending kindergarten at Gainesville Homeschool Academy and completely loved it. She made many friends and thrived in that environment. The following fall, Caleb and Jesse joined her there: Caleb in fifth grade and Jesse in third. They had the most amazing teachers and have made what I believe will be lifelong friendships. The Lord truly blessed us by guiding us to GHA.

There are probably as many opinions about which homeschool curriculum to use as there are homeschooling families. A quick Internet search will reveal that there are untold numbers of websites and blogs and online stores for homeschoolers. My advice is this: Do your homework; ask several homeschooling families what curriculum works for them without relying on just one as I had. Discover your kids' learning styles, and fit your teaching methods around those styles, as much as possible. My big boys are active learners as are most boys, so when they were little, I would let them jump around on the couch while they were doing their spelling lessons. To this day, they both are amazing spellers. Also, try to keep things somewhat structured and orderly. Having some routines that become habits, but that still allow for the freedom to change things, if necessary, will help keep you saner and your children more productive. Find what works for your family, and don't be afraid to try new things. I was afraid of trying something new in those first few years, so I stuck with the same boring curriculum that I had used from the first day. I wish that I had stepped out and used different methods and different curriculum; I believe that our experiences would have been much more positive early on. Also, if something isn't working mid-year, don't be afraid to switch to something new. The peace in your home is worth the extra effort and expense involved in choosing something different.

Our homeschool academy ends with fifth grade, and my Caleb was in fifth grade when he started there in 2012. He loved it so much that I knew he wouldn't be content just doing school with me full time for sixth grade, so I got together with two other homeschooling families, and over several months' time we made all of the preparations to start a homeschool academy for middle schoolers. We call it Legacy Homeschool Academy. We started school in August 2013 with six sweet little students. I'm so thankful for the Lord's guidance.

We have chosen some wonderful resources for the middle school academy that we started. For science and history, we're using some amazing curriculum from Answers in Genesis: God's Design for Science and History Revealed. I highly recommend both! We're using some of the readers that Sonlight recommends to complement the history curriculum, and each student has a book of centuries (timeline in a book) from Simply Charlotte Mason into which they record important people or events in the appropriate century. We use ACSI for math, and we do nature studies, art appreciation, memorize long Scripture passages, write research papers, and many other activities that enhance their learning. It's a comprehensive education, and the kids love it!

In addition to the homeschool academy, our three older kids have all begun taking karate and piano classes in the last couple of years. As we began each of these activities, we felt the Lord's hand guiding us and opening the doors. The karate teacher is a strong Christian, as is the kids' piano teacher. Our children have grown and matured and are developing amazing life skills.

However, each activity that we've added for the kids has come at a great price to our budget. Our youngest isn't involved in any costly activities yet, but we know that it won't be long until he is ready to begin some things. The homeschool academy, piano classes, and karate for the three older kids cost us over $12,000 each year. That's a major expense on a teacher's salary. I'm no longer keeping Trevor's niece because she started public school this fall, and my part-time from home job brings in very little income. Because the economy has been so depressed for the last several years, Trevor has endured multiple pay cuts as a public school teacher, and at this point, his salary is down around 10 percent due to various forms of cuts.

We've had to do some major surgery to our budget to be able to afford to educate our children and to provide the enrichment activities that we've chosen. We have cut out frivolous spending as much as possible; I coupon extensively to keep our grocery costs to a minimum (more on that later); and we have very little extra to add to our savings right now.

I get nervous sometimes when I think about how we will replace our cars or our roof or our refrigerator in the future when they wear out. Just this year, our main level heat pump went out, and it cost $4,000 to replace the system. We had to pull from our savings to cover it, and we don't know when we'll be able to replace that money.

We've been slammed with medical expenses for our kids this year: pneumonia, hernia surgery, stitches, allergy testing, x-rays, hearing tests, medicines. Our health insurance rates increased 40 percent this year, and our plan pays very little until high deductibles are met. We are looking at braces for one, maybe two of our kids in the near future, as well.

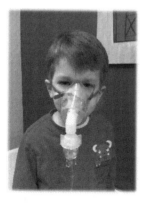

NOAH'S BREATHING TREATMENT FOR BRONCHITIS/PNEUMONIA LATE 2012/EARLY 2013

CAROLINE GETTING STITCHES SPRING 2013

This is a very financially tight season for us, but we believe that we are doing for our family what the Lord wants at this time, and He will provide what we need when we need it. When we answered the Lord's call to remain debt free the rest of our lives, didn't that mean that He would bless us with financial riches? No, it didn't. We had hoped that He would open up heaven and pour out a huge financial gift on us so we could build our house quickly, but it didn't happen. No, we worked hard and scrimped and saved for several years in the jobs that He provided for us, building and finishing our house as we could afford it.

The Lord knows that I am willing to work hard to earn extra income, but my time is very limited homeschooling four children and managing our household right now. My commitment is to raise the children God has given us, earning a little income as He provides opportunities. Trevor has willingly taken on several extra school projects as they have become available, and those have helped tremendously with the kids' expenses, but for the first time in our entire journey, we feel like we're just scraping by. There were times of plenty in years past when the house was finished and the kids were small, but this is a lean time when the kids' expenses are high and the income has shrunk.

Does this mean that God has abandoned us? Absolutely not. Can we take the prosperous times and reject the tight ones? No, because He has a purpose for every season of our lives. He was not surprised by how expensive it would be to raise four children. He has promised to provide for us, and we take Him at His Word. We believe that our part is to work hard in the opportunities that He gives us and to focus on the task of raising our children for His glory; He will take care of the rest.

We try to focus on all of our blessings when the discontentment begins to creep in, and it does creep in. We get frustrated with the economy, with pay cuts, with medical expenses, with unexpected home repairs, with the price of gas, but we have to remind ourselves that we have a home, cars that run, plenty of food, a wonderful church, amazing friends and family, a beautiful world to enjoy, and a Savior who loves us and gave His very life so that we could be with Him one day. All of the things of this world will pass away eventually, but what matters for eternity are the things that we do for the Lord and His Kingdom. May our focus be on how we can lead others into His Kingdom and help them become more like Jesus, starting with our own children.

14

COUPONING

"You will eat the fruit of your labor; blessings and prosperity will be yours." (Psalm 128:2)

When our Noah was born in 2008, we were going to church with a family very much like ours—three boys and a girl with similar ages to our children. They were home-schoolers also, so we had a lot in common. The wife Julie used to comment occasionally about how cheaply she got things through couponing. She piqued my interest, because I'm always up for a good deal. Our grocery budget at that time had been inching up with each new child that we had added, so I needed to do something to cut costs. Buying generic brands at the grocery store just wasn't making enough difference.

I asked my friend Julie if she would show me how to coupon, so she told me how to get started and gave me many good ideas. I was most interested in learning how to "do" CVS, as Julie talked about all of the free things that she often got there. CVS, a drugstore chain, has an awesome rewards program that can potentially net free or almost free stuff, and even a few money maker items.

I discovered two amazing websites for couponers and deal hunters, and I owe most of my savings to the two mag-

nificent ladies who run those sites. They are SouthernSav-
ers.com and MoneySavingMom.com. There are scores of
couponing websites online, but these two are my favorites
and the ones that I have used far and above any others. Both
sites are run by sweet Christian homeschooling mamas who
make it their mission to help other families save money, and
I will be forever grateful for their encouragement and support.

I started buying the Sunday newspapers so I would have
the coupons that I needed for the deals. I learned that my
small-town newspaper gets far fewer coupons than the *Atlanta Journal-Constitution*, so I began buying the AJC each
week. I learned later that companies offer multitudes of coupons that I can print online from home, also. I prepared my
coupons for my first CVS trip. I was so excited that I could
hardly sleep.

CVS shopping involves buying products that produce
"Extra Care Bucks" (ECBs or Extra Bucks). Extra Bucks are
CVS "dollars" that can be used almost like cash to buy other
items that produce Extra Bucks, essentially "rolling" the
bucks and getting things for free or almost free. When you
use a coupon on the item that produces Extra Bucks, the coupon reduces the cost of the item up front, and fewer Extra
Bucks are required to pay for it. Occasionally, CVS offers
products that are "free after Extra Bucks," meaning that you
get the same amount back in Extra Bucks that you paid for
it. If a coupon is used on the item, it becomes a money
maker.

Here's an example: Suppose contact solution is on sale

for $7.99, and I will receive $7.99 in ECBs if I buy the contact solution. I have a $1 coupon for that brand of contact solution, so when I buy it I will owe $6.99 plus tax. I use $6.99 ECBs that I have from prior purchases to pay for the balance. I receive on my receipt an ECB for $7.99, which is $1 more than I paid. I can then use that $7.99 to purchase other items that also produce ECBs.

My first CVS trip was a memorable experience. It's best to start really small and figure it all out, but that's just not me. When I do something, I jump in with both feet. I planned my trip based on what was on sale at the time and gathered my coupons together. I went in, put all of the products in my shopping cart, and tried to separate them into which items I would buy first, second, third, and so on, and I went to check out. Thankfully, the store wasn't crowded when I was there, because my check-out took a *really* long time. I did multiple transactions to roll my ECBs, with the goal of paying the least out of pocket. As I was standing at the counter, I was trying to break down each transaction based on how many ECBs had just printed on the previous transaction. I think I drove the poor cashier crazy. I didn't know what I was doing, but she was so patient with me, and I learned so much during that trip that I was hooked!

In the almost five years since that first CVS trip, I have saved literally thousands of dollars by couponing. I shop now at CVS and sometimes Rite Aid drug stores where I get virtually all of our toiletries, paper towels, toilet paper, laundry detergent, vitamins, soft drinks, and other products very cheaply. However, in recent years Rite Aid's coupon policy has become much less coupon-friendly, so I focus most of my drug store time at CVS. For groceries, I shop at the Kroger and Publix stores near our house. Up to now, both grocery stores have doubled coupons up to 50 cents, but Kroger stores have just ended their coupon doubling. This makes me very sad.

Publix has a number of "Buy One Get One Free" sales each week. In this area, that means the product is actually half price. You don't really buy one at full price and get one free. When a coupon is paired with that sale item, it can make for an awesome deal, added to that the many Publix store coupons that are provided. Publix allows you to "stack" a store coupon with a manufacturer coupon on the same item, and you can net free or almost free stuff. Cha-ching! For more detailed tutorials on couponing and for up-to-date coupon matchups for various stores, feel free to visit Southern-Savers.com and MoneySavingMom.com.

One of the goals of a serious couponer is to build up a stockpile of non-perishable products so that buying those items at full price will never be necessary. When an item is at its lowest price (or close to it), I buy enough of it to last for several weeks until it's on sale again. Sales typically run in cycles, so most items will be a "stock-up price" occasionally. The key is finding out what the stock-up price is for the items that you buy and then buying enough to last until the next time you find it around that price. It takes time and practice really to "get" couponing, and some people never really understand it or want to understand it. For us, it is a necessity, but I also enjoy the thrill of saving money.

I began to build my stockpile, and within a few months

I had a pretty decent one going. Because we have a full base-ment apartment/in-law suite that is unoccupied right now, we use that area to hold the stockpile. The kitchen cabinets are full of cleaning supplies, canned goods, and non-perish-able items like rice, mac and cheese, pasta, pasta sauces, nuts, parmesan cheese, cereals, cocoa powder, dessert mixes, snacks, pickles, tea bags, coffee, sugar, condiments, juice boxes, and many other non-perishables. Toiletries such as dental floss, mouth wash, toothpaste, hair products, soaps and razors fill the medicine cabinets and a small stand-alone cabinet in the basement bathroom. The basement laundry room houses the stockpile of paper towels, toilet paper, laun-dry detergent, and fabric softeners. The basement linen closet holds light bulbs, baby wipes, facial tissues, and hand sanitizer. A curio cabinet in the basement living room is full of hand soaps and air fresheners and fragrant candles. We also have a couple of stand-alone freezers and a refrigera-tor/freezer in the basement that hold refrigerated and frozen items that I buy at their stock-up prices, and we just bought a quarter of a steer, so we'll have fresh, organic beef for quite a while.

We don't take stockpiling to the extreme that you might see on some reality TV shows (hundreds of sticks of deodor-ant and so on). We certainly don't want to be hoarders and rob others of the opportunity to get a good deal as well. Yet, we probably would be in pretty good position to survive for a few months on what we have if something catastrophic happened in the world. For that, I'm thankful.

For us, couponing has been a huge blessing. For our

family of six, we budget $250 each month for groceries, toiletries, and paper products. As food prices have risen dramatically in recent years with the distressed economy and outrageous gas prices, we have had plenty in spite of those rising prices. Interestingly, I buy almost all name-brand items now. We buy very few store-brand items anymore—only things such as milk and bread—because sales plus coupons generally produce better prices on name-brand products.

Also, and very importantly, couponing has allowed us to be generous *far* beyond what we would have been able to afford before. Several times since I started couponing, situations have arisen in our community in which people needed a hand. A family's house burned, a friend's husband died suddenly, and we have been able to throw together big boxes of food, toiletries, and cleaning supplies to give away without a dent to our budget. I also have enjoyed putting together many pretty gift baskets of special items for people who have had babies or are sick or as a thank you or for Christmas. Also, our church has been doing a monthly outreach for many years to one of the housing projects in our town. We provide six items that people can't buy with their food stamps—paper towels, toilet paper, dishwashing liquid, bleach, toothpaste, and bath soap. Another big blessing of my couponing is that I can often get several of these items (dishwashing liquid, soap, and toothpaste) free or very cheaply. I can contribute to the monthly ministry of our church with very little out of pocket expense. I'm so thankful for the Lord's wisdom in this area of our financial lives.

15

STEWARDSHIP

"Whoever can be trusted with very little can also be trusted with much, and whoever is dishonest with very little will also be dishonest with much." (Luke 16:10)

Contrary to what many church members might think, stewardship isn't a fund-raising campaign for church expenses. Stewardship involves being a wise manager of the resources that God entrusts to us. First Chronicles 29:11-12 tells us, "....for everything in heaven and earth is yours. Yours, O Lord, is the kingdom; you are exalted as head over all. Wealth and honor come from you; you are the ruler of all things. In your hands are strength and power to exalt and give strength to all. Now, our God, we give you thanks, and praise your glorious name." Psalm 24:1 says, "The earth is the Lord's, and everything in it, the world, and all who live in it."

These passages tell us that God is the owner of all things. We are merely stewards or managers of His property here on earth. Trevor and I believe that this principle of stewardship, the idea that none of us really "owns" anything, is the most important financial principle taught in Scripture. Until a person comes to grips with this, he or she will never truly understand money and wealth.

How we handle God's possessions is significantly important to Him. We can't take anything with us when we die. Does it please Him when we squander His resources on excessive interest payments or on wasteful spending? Probably not. Larry Burkett used to say that we have enough resources in this nation to fund The Great Commission worldwide, if we would just get out of debt and direct those extra funds into Kingdom work.

America is the most generous nation on earth. In 2008 *World Magazine* reported that, "A new study by the Hudson Institute's Center for Global Prosperity reported that Americans account for 45 percent of all philanthropic giving worldwide. Not only is that significantly more than any other nation on earth, it's also dramatically more on a per capita basis. One example: The average American gives 14 times more to charity than the average Italian." This came as no surprise to Arthur C. Brooks, a fellow at the Hudson Institute. "Americans give at least twice as much as anyone else," Brooks said. In addition, he added, "And we're giving now more than ever before."[1]

However, even though the U.S. is the most generous nation on earth, and even though God's people are generally the most generous Americans, giving among U.S. Christians falls far short of what Scripture reveals that it should be. As Larry often reported—and the numbers have changed little today—the average giving among U.S. Christians is only about two to three percent of their gross income.

---

[1] http://www.worldmag.com/2008/07/aid_and_comfort

In the New Testament there is a lot of teaching on being generous but very little on what exact amount we should give. The tithe (literally 10 percent), while mentioned often in the Old Testament, is rarely mentioned in the New Testament. Larry's belief was that such teaching was unnecessary. Remember who Jesus' main audience was: the Jews. Tithing was a principle that Jews understood very well. It is how the Pharisees drew their income. In Matthew 23, where Jesus mentioned the tithe, he pointed out the Pharisees' hypocrisy. He noted that, while they tithed down to the smallest amount, they neglected more important things such as justice, mercy, and faith. However, notice that Christ did not correct or condemn their giving. Ten percent was the minimum standard set forth in Scripture when it came to what God's people were to give.

It's not that God needs anyone's money, and it's not that any particular amount is going to make you righteous in God's eyes or secure you blessings from heaven, in spite of what you may have heard from some Christians. God owns "the cattle on a thousand hills." What He wants is us. We don't give because He has needs. We give out of our need to recognize His ownership and authority over our lives. As Larry also noted, God isn't going to judge the amount you give but the heart with which you give it.

When Trevor and I got married and I established our budget, he was a bit taken aback at the amount we were going to be giving to our church, our tithe. He had never tithed before, so it was hard for him to wrap his mind around simply giving away 10 percent of his gross income each

month, rather than $25 here and there as he was used to do-
ing, but as he worked through the Bible study and took to
heart God's financial principles, he understood the importance of that tangible expression of God's ownership of
everything we had. As we quickly learned, when we are
faithful to give back that portion of what God entrusts to us,
He makes the other 90 percent stretch to meet our needs, and
then some.

One of the things that has been important to Trevor and
me through the years is extra giving. For us, this means giving above the 10 percent of gross income that goes to our
church, giving "offerings" to Christian organizations that are
working to fulfill The Great Commission. We have a category in our budget called "Contributions" that is separate
from our Tithe category. Even before we were out of debt,
we were giving monthly above our tithe to a missionary couple with Youth With a Mission, to Promise Keepers, to our
local crisis pregnancy center, to Compassion International,
and to our local Christian radio station. Through the years,
we added monthly contributions to ministries such as Christian Financial Concepts, Focus on the Family, Alliance De-
fending Freedom, Good News Clinics, Answers in Genesis,
Adventures in Missions, Helping Hands Foreign Missions,
and Wallbuilders. Occasionally, we give to individuals in
our community as needs arise, although we are cautious
about this because we have been scammed more than once.

At one point, we were giving close to 20 percent of our
gross income away each month when the kids were very
small and our house was completed. In recent years we've
had to reduce some of our extra giving, partly because of

Trevor's deep pay cuts and partly because, as our children have gotten older, the cost to educate, feed, and clothe them has grown significantly. We feel, however, that the Christian education of our children is perhaps one of our most important investments into God's Kingdom here on earth. When our children are grown and as Trevor's income is restored, we have committed to redirect more of our resources back into those ministries that are important to our hearts.

Our monthly monetary gifts to the various ministries aren't extravagant—most average around $25 each—but over several years' time, those amounts add up. We have felt so blessed to be able to partner with these para-church ministries and with our church to further God's purposes around the world.

Stewardship is a pretty big responsibility. As we recognize and understand that God owns it all, we can see how important it is to be excellent managers of His resources. Of course, He wants us to care for ourselves and our families, but His heart is generous and He wants us to be generous with others, doing our part to further His Kingdom here on earth.

I love the story of R.G. LeTourneau. He invented and produced earth-moving machines (bulldozers, scrapers, dump wagons, logging equipment, the electric wheel, and many others). In fact, his company produced 70 percent of all of the army's earth-moving equipment in World War II. LeTourneau had very humble beginnings, but he became a multi-millionaire, eventually giving away 90 percent of his profits to God's work and living on the remaining 10 percent. His autobiography *Mover of Men and Mountains* is an amazing story, and LeTourneau said of his generous giving, "I shovel it out and God shovels it back, but God has a bigger shovel."[2] May we be "moved" and inspired to be open-handed with the resources that God entrusts to us, too.

---

[2] http://edhird.blogspot.com/2007/12/rg-letourneau-model-of-generosity.html

16

WHAT DOES IT ALL MEAN? (OKAY, YOU'RE DEBT FREE, SO WHAT?)

"The Lord is my Shepherd, I lack nothing." (Psalm 23:1)

My dear husband graciously agreed to write this last chapter, and I hope you enjoy it as much as I did. Trevor loves to write and has been writing opinion columns for various newspapers and online sites for many years now. The Lord has blessed him with much wisdom, and I'm thankful that he was willing to share it here.

In the *How to Manage Your Money* Bible study that was so influential to us early in our marriage, the late Larry Burkett noted, "In the end, the only thing that is going to matter is what you did in the name of Jesus. Everything else is just wood, hay, and stubble to be burned up."[1] Being debt free is a good thing, some may even say a great thing, but it is not the best thing.

God didn't put Michelle and me on this path simply for our benefit. As is typical when He asks us to do hard things, it isn't all about us and what we want. In the beginning, I did *not* want to build a home debt free. I knew well that, unless tens-of-thousands of dollars suddenly fell into our laps, the

---

[1] Burkett, Larry, *How to Manage Your Money*, Chicago, Moody Press, 1991, session 2 video tape.

money required to build a home was going to take us some time to accumulate. I'm not a very patient person. This has gotten me into trouble more than once and has sometimes made life difficult for those closest to me. Looking at our budget at the time, I was in no way excited about how long I imagined it would take us to build a home without borrowing money.

Is that not the great lure of debt? It makes "affording" things that we don't really have the money to buy so easy. Larry always said if you can't afford to save and buy something, then you can't really afford it. Sadly, many Americans have recently learned the hard way what they could not really afford.

When it comes to personal finances, the Great Recession has certainly gained the focus of an otherwise ADD-afflicted America. A Barna Group report in January of 2008, just as the Great Recession was beginning in the U.S., declared that "Americans are troubled by a diverse palette of concerns. Three types of issues are of particular concern, perceived as 'major' problems facing the country."[2] Leading the way, with 78 percent listing it as a "major problem," was the personal debt of individual Americans.

The Great Recession, just as with any other, had many contributing factors. However, most experts agree that this recession, which began in late 2007, was caused mostly by the so-called subprime mortgage crisis. Blame for this crisis

---

[2] https://www.barna.org/culture-articles/50-americans-describe-their-moral-and-social-concerns-including-abortion-and-homosexuality

has been laid at the feet of various entities.

Whoever is to blame, tens of millions of Americans are suffering as a result. In my state of Georgia, according to the *Atlanta Journal-Constitution*, the National Bankruptcy Research Center reported that between January and November of 2009, one in 50 Georgia households declared bankruptcy. Nationwide, during the same period, personal bankruptcies were up 32 percent.[3] As the *Wall Street Journal* recently put it, "never...underestimate [U.S. consumers'] willingness to spend beyond their means."[4]

By 2010, the personal debt of Americans reached epic proportions. In early 2010, David Beim, a professor at the Columbia Business School noted that "currently consumers owe $13 trillion [while the] GDP is $13 trillion. That is a ton."[5] In other words, U.S. household debt reached a level that was equal to the total U.S. economy. According to Beim, this happened only once before in U.S. history: 1929.

Speaking in the early 1990s, when the median price of a home was about $108,000, Larry Burkett asked, "What do you think the price of a house would be if you couldn't borrow to buy a house? Do you think a $108,000 house would sell for $108,000 if you couldn't sell it to anybody with a loan?" His answer: "No way. Nor would it sell for $58,000.

---

[3] http://www.ajc.com/news/business/georgia-personal-bankruptcies-rate-third-highest-i/nQbM2/

[4] http://online.wsj.com/news/articles/SB124449816432295655

[5] http://hnn.us/article/67279

It would probably sell for around $28,000. Everything above that we've built into it through debt."[6] I wonder how much debt is built into the current median price of a home, which is now around $220,000.

Our attitude and behavior toward debt have made practically every large ticket item in our culture more expensive. As Ken Blackwell of the Family Research Council recently wrote, "We have become a culture addicted to instant gratification and a fixation on the material. Increasingly, concepts such as duty, self-denial, hard work, delayed gratification, and patience have been swept away."[7] In other words, we are a culture addicted to debt.

Of course, the vast majority of debt held by Americans is in their mortgages. According to the Federal Reserve, at the end of the first quarter of this year, the outstanding mortgage debt of Americans was just over $13 trillion.[8] While this is down from $14.4 trillion at the end of 2009, Americans are significantly "underwater" with their homes. This means that Americans owe lenders about $1 trillion more than their homes are worth.

In his best seller, *The Coming Economic Earthquake*, Larry may not have foreseen the subprime mortgage crisis,

---

[6] Burkett, Larry, *How to Manage Your Money*, Chicago, Moody Press, 1991, session 1 video tape.

[7] http://www.realclearpolitics.com/articles/2008/10/addicted_to_debt.html

[8] http://www.federalreserve.gov/econresdata/releases/mortoutstand/current.htm

but writing about mortgages, home equity loans, and easy lines of credit, he did note that, "Clearly many American homeowners have transferred the wealth stored in their homes to the lenders. In this case, it leaves both in jeopardy. Given the wrong set of circumstances, the homeowners will default, leaving the banks with huge inventories of homes they can't sell."[9]

Of course, we now know that "the wrong set of circumstances," became "the perfect storm" for many homeowners, lenders, and the government.

The deep indebtedness of Americans goes far beyond mortgage debt. Consider the amount of automobile debt Americans have. Bad automobile debt also contributed to the credit crisis that sent the U.S. into the Great Recession. With correct foresight, the *L.A. Times* reported in late 2007 that, with the number of risky car loans approaching the same level as the number of risky home loans, a new credit crunch was on the horizon for Americans.[10] In late 2012, Americans still owed a near record $750 billion on auto loans.

Automobile debt is some of the worst debt that most of us carry. Given that many, especially young, Americans view an automobile as a significant status symbol, an auto loan is typically the first significant debt Americans take on. Many spend much more on a car than is necessary or than

---

[9] Burkett, Larry, *The Coming Economic Earthquake*, Chicago, Moody Press, 1994, page 111.

[10] Bensinger, Ken, *LA Times*, Los Angeles, December 30, 2007.

they can really afford, and thus the cycle of deep indebtedness often begins in the late teens for some Americans.

Many Americans are so desperate for that new car that, as ABC News reported in 2008, nearly half of all new-car buyers are signing off on loans that are longer than six years.[11] Given that cars lose their value rapidly (about 18 percent in the first year alone), such loans end up "underwater" very quickly.

Along with homes and automobiles, many Americans are also saddled with crippling student loan debt. While student loan debt is often considered "good debt," in that it often leads to significantly more income over a lifetime, most recent college graduates are finding that not to be the case. According to a 2011 survey, 53.6 percent of bachelor's degree-holders under the age of 25 were unemployed or underemployed, working lower-skilled jobs such as waiter, retail clerk, bartender, and the like, making little or no use of their college education.[12] What's more, in 2011 *Time* magazine reported on a study revealing that 85 percent of new college graduates are moving back in with their parents.[13]

Of course, student loan debt is greatly due to the astronomical rise of the cost of a college education. The cost of tuition and fees has increased faster than even healthcare

---

[11] http://abcnews.go.com/GMA/MellodyHobson/story?id=4170624

[12] http://usatoday30.usatoday.com/news/nation/story/2012-04-22/college-grads-jobless/54473426/1

[13] http://newsfeed.time.com/2011/05/10/survey-85-of-new-college-grads-moving-back-in-with-mom-and-dad/

costs. According to the Department of Education, if these trends continue, by 2016 the cost of a public college will have more than doubled in just 15 years.[14] University of Tennessee law professor, Glenn Harlan Reynolds, in his book *The Higher Education Bubble*, reports that, with the easy availability of federal funds (in other words, "easy" debt), tuition and fees have gone up over 440 percent in the last 30 years.[15]

In late 2011, for the first time in U.S. history, student loan debt topped $1 trillion. Americans now owe more on their student loans than on their credit cards. Truly, debt has become far too acceptable—a way of life, even—in American culture.

You've seen the ads on television and heard them on the radio. There is a whole industry now devoted to "helping" Americans with their debt. Some of these are legitimate; some are not, but one thing is clear: Such an industry exists only because of the vast number of Americans who find themselves in trouble, or at least looking for answers when facing our culture of debt.

"An absolute principle of economics," wrote Larry in his best seller, is that, "No one, government or otherwise, can spend more than he or she makes indefinitely. At some

---

[14] http://www.nytimes.com/2012/05/13/business/student-loans-weighing-down-a-generation-with-heavy-debt.html?_r=0

[15] http://www.amazon.com/Higher-Education-Bubble-Encounter-Broadside-ebook/dp/B0088Q9TAU

point the compounding interest will consume all the money in the world." He added that, "With so many variables in the economy, the one non-variable is this: What you own belongs to you and not to a lender."[16]

Early on, as God was beginning to get my attention and prepare me for what was coming, one of the Scriptures that most spoke to me was Proverbs 22:7. It reads, "The rich rule over the poor, and the borrower is servant to the lender." If you've ever suffered under the burden of significant debt, you know exactly what this verse is talking about: The bills, the phone calls, the stress, the anger, the frustration, and in many cases, bankruptcy and divorce. I believe that there are tens of millions of Americans, including millions of Christians, who understand this verse all too well.

As Michelle has already written, in my young adult days I was eager to fill my life with what I felt like I had missed out on while I was a child. Like millions of others, I overspent. Because Michelle entered my life, things never got to the point where I needed counseling. Larry personally counseled hundreds, maybe thousands, of individuals and couples. He always noted that whatever their financial difficulties, his clients' problems were never ultimately financial, and neither were mine.

When describing a typical counseling session, Larry often noted that the couple or individual was not having financial problems; they were having financial symptoms,

---

[16] Burkett, Larry, *The Coming Economic Earthquake*, Chicago, Moody Press, 1994, page 181.

symptoms that reflected deeper problems in their lives. In other words, money and how we use it is not a problem in anyone's life. "It is a symbol, or an indicator of problems. It is the visible indicator of who we are and what we believe."[17]

The use of money is a great barometer for anyone's life. This is why Jesus often used money or wealth in His parables. According to Larry, to teach people about the Kingdom of God, Jesus used money in about two-thirds of His parables. Why did He do this? Because, even 2,000 years ago money was something that spoke to almost everyone. Consider the Parable of the Talents from Matthew 25. In this parable, a very wealthy man ("master") leaves home and entrusts varying amounts of his estate, in the form of "talents," to three of his servants. One servant got five talents, the second got two talents, and the third servant received a single talent. A talent was a unit of weight (about 80 pounds). When it was used as a measure of money, it was the value of that weight in silver. Thus, each servant received a substantial amount of money. By some estimates, a talent was worth about 20 years' wages for the average worker.

After a long absence, upon his return, the master asks for an account from each of the servants for how they have handled his estate. The two who received five and two talents had each doubled their amount. He praised them and rewarded them both. The third servant reported to having buried his talent in the ground, earning nothing for his mas-

---

[17] Burkett, Larry, *How to Manage Your Money*, Chicago, Moody Press, 1991, session 1 video tape.

ter. The master rebuked him ("You wicked and slothful servant.") and sent him away to be punished.

I believe that the message here is similar to that of the Parable of the Shrewd Manager in Luke 16:10-11. "Whoever can be trusted with very little can also be trusted with much, and whoever is dishonest with very little will also be dishonest with much. So if you have not been trustworthy in handling worldly wealth, who will trust you with true riches?" In other words, if we can't handle our worldly possessions, how can we be entrusted with eternal ones? God, who is the Owner of all things, often uses His earthly resources as a barometer, not for Himself, but so that we will see where our hearts are when considering earthly things vs. eternal things.

As Michelle noted in the previous chapter, we believe that the principle of stewardship is the most important financial principle taught in Scripture. A steward is a manager of another's property. Once I came to grips with my role as a steward of God's property, our lives were never the same. The idea of stewardship goes well beyond our household budget. "You are not your own; you were bought at a price. Therefore honor God with your bodies" (see 1 Corinthians 6:19-20). Our bodies, our minds, our talents and abilities, these all came from God. He is our Creator. He owns us. He purchased us with the blood of His Son. We literally owe Him everything. Therefore, honoring God with our finances is one of the least things we can do.

However, even though I was a Christian, it was no small or easy step for me to turn over my finances to Him completely, especially when that meant building a home debt free. However, God's call on our lives was very clear, and I had to choose: Do it His way or mine.

Throughout Scripture, we see accounts of where God calls individuals to do things with which they are uncomfortable. Whether Abraham, Joseph, Moses, David, Esther, many of the Prophets, or several of the disciples, time and again we see God asking of people what, at the time, seems quite impossible. Thus, doubts and fear rear their ugly heads.

Of course, near the climax of Scripture just prior to going to the cross, Jesus Christ Himself prayed to His Father, "[I]f it is possible, may this cup be taken from me." Not that Christ had doubt or fear, but clearly his path weighed heavily upon Him.

This certainly is not to say that our little tale is on par with such giants of Scripture. Throughout time—in fact, most every day—God has done, and continues to do, countless such things with people to build His Kingdom. Usually we never hear of these events. In fact, as you examine your own life and the lives of those closest to you, you can probably find similar situations; some are more significant than others.

In many ways, choosing to follow God is a daily decision. Do we listen to that "still small voice"? Do we pray for that friend, coworker, or stranger as He leads us? Do we give when we know we're supposed to, even though we would rather spend on ourselves? Are we faithfully generous, even in the hard times? Do we stop in our daily routine to help those in need? A life walking with Jesus is certainly not always going to be a comfortable or an easy one. Anyone teaching or preaching this is a deceiver.

Do you think what God has called you to do is difficult? There are some who are to be obedient "even unto death." History proves this. God knows our limits. He knows us better than we know ourselves. He knows well of what we are capable.

Our path was literally filled with blood, sweat, and tears. Certainly there was much good fruit upon the way and we hope much more. However, as I noted above, this call upon our lives was not only to bless us. Quite early on, I felt that God was doing this to use us to help build His Kingdom. Isn't that what it's all about? Are not our good deeds meant to be more than just nice things we do to meet someone else's needs?

Consider for a moment all of the miracles performed by Jesus that are recorded in the New Testament. He turned water to wine and healed the sick, including the blind, the leprous, the deaf, the crippled, and the mute. He cast out demons and calmed storms. He fed thousands with a handful of food, walked on water, and raised the dead. Wondrous things, no doubt, but why? Why did Jesus do these things? Many Christians fail to ask this, and if they do, they often arrive at the wrong conclusions. Jesus was not merely being "nice."

What many people seem to want out of "religion," especially Christianity and its followers, is simply nice "do-gooders" who go about their business without causing any trouble. The greatest of Christ's miracles recorded in Scripture was raising someone from the dead. There are three recorded instances of this occurring. This was not done merely out of "niceness," only to save the lives of those who had died. They would, after all (with apologies to James Bond), "die another day." His ultimate goal was to give them everlasting life.

This could be said of every miracle Christ performed. It is true that He healed, fed, and cast out demons because of His great love for those in need. However, these acts alone did not save anyone. Those healed of one disease or sickness would someday die of another. Those fed would someday be hungry again. Christ's ultimate goal was to bring people into His Kingdom.

God became man not simply to improve us, but to make us into new creatures. As Ravi Zacharias says often, "Jesus didn't come into the world to make bad people good. He came into the world to make dead people live."

In the words of my pastor, Michelle's dad, God wants us to be "dangerous"—to the enemy, that is. That was, and is, our mission. In a culture that is consumed with a lifestyle of debt, which, as Michelle has already pointed out, so often hinders the work of the Kingdom, it would be quite dangerous to the schemes of Satan for large numbers of God's people to be free of the burden of financial debt.

I've always said that our path was a calling. Our debt-free lifestyle is how God chose to use us to help build His Kingdom. His message of stewardship and financial wisdom is, just as the rest of His Word, timeless and beneficial to all. God has a plan and a purpose for each of us. As Larry pointed out in the *How to Manage Your Money* Bible study, this world is not our home. We need to think more about our eternity. Whatever we will be with God is being established right now. It can't be altered once we leave this life. To a great extent, we are being measured by how we manage money.[18] May God richly bless you and make His face shine upon you. May He give you His peace and wisdom as He seeks to make you more like His Son.

---

[18] Burkett, Larry, *How to Manage Your Money*, Chicago, Moody Press, 1991, session 1 video tape.

A FINAL WORD

Thank you for taking time out of your life to read our story. We hope that you've been encouraged, blessed, and drawn closer to the Lord somehow through our experiences. We've opened ourselves up, bared our souls, and made ourselves vulnerable because we hope and pray that God will use what we've done to lead others closer to Him. Since the beginning of our journey, our desire has been that God would do mighty things in His Kingdom through what He asked us to do. We're living proof that God's principles are true, they work, and they are given for our good.

If you have made it to this point and you're wondering how to have a personal relationship with Jesus or you're not sure whether you will spend eternity with Him, we encourage you to take a moment right now to give your life to Him. God loves you with an everlasting love (Jeremiah 31:3), He sent His Son Jesus to take the penalty for your sins and ours (John 3:16), and He desperately wants a relationship with you. Simply talk to the Lord; repent of your sins (turn from them), confess to the Lord that you are a sinner, and believe that Jesus died for you (Mark 1:15). Jesus said in John 14:6 that He is the *only* way to the Father—the Way, the Truth, and the Life. He is our only hope.

If you made a decision just now to follow Christ, we would love to hear about it! Please contact us through our website, KingdomCrossing.com. Also, we encourage you to get involved with a strong Bible-teaching church in your area so that you can grow in your relationship with Christ and help lead others to Him.

We pray many blessings on you and your family always!

In Christ,

Trevor and Michelle

SUGGESTED RESOURCES

As we've walked this journey of paying off debt, building a house, homeschooling, and couponing, and we've expanded our family size from two to six, we've gleaned a lot of wisdom from various people and organizations. I'd like to share some of those resources with you here.

Budgeting/God's Principles of Managing Money:

Crown Financial Ministries www.crown.org

Howard Dayton www.compass.org

Dave Ramsey www.daveramsey.com

Mvelopes www.finicity.com

Couponing:

Southern Savers www.southernsavers.com

Money Saving Mom www.moneysavingmom.com

Debt Management Assistance:

CredAbility www.CredAbility.org

Investing:

Austin Pryor www.soundmindinvesting.com

Ron Blue www.ronblue.com

Kingdom Advisors www.kingdomadvisors.com

Family Resources/General Bible Counsel:

Ken Ham www.answersingenesis.org

World Magazine www.worldmag.com

James Dobson www.familytalk.org

Focus on the Family www.focusonthefamily.org

Promise Keepers www.promisekeepers.org

Wallbuilders www.wallbuilders.com

Homeschooling:

Simply Charlotte Mason www.simplycharlottemason.com

The Old Schoolhouse Magazine www.thehomeschool-magazine.com

Sonlight www.sonlight.com

Answers in Genesis www.answersingenesis.org

Homeschool Legal Defense Association www.hslda.org

Donna Young www.donnayoung.org

Christian Book Distributors www.christianbook.com

One last resource that is near to my heart is my husband's website, www.TrevorGrantThomas.com. Trevor has been writing Christian commentary for the last dozen or so years. His works have been published on Real Clear Politics, Real Clear Religion, Real Clear Science (one of the few ever to achieve this "Real Clear" trifecta), US Action News, American Thinker, and Center for a Just Society. His columns have been in our local newspapers, *The Atlanta Journal-Constitution* and *The Gainesville Times*. I'm super-proud of his thoughtful commentary, and I hope you'll check it out.

ABOUT THE AUTHORS

 Michelle Thomas is a Christ follower, wife to Trevor, and homeschooling mom to Caleb, Jesse, Caroline, and Noah. Married in 1998, Michelle and Trevor found themselves renting a small apartment and coping with $25,000 in debt. They developed a budget and began paying off their debts. Meanwhile, they heard God's call on their lives never to go into debt again—for anything.

They saved money and built their home debt free over the course of a few years, have since paid cash for several used vehicles, and now are investing a significant portion of their income into the Christian education of their children.

Trevor teaches high school mathematics in Gainesville, Georgia. In his spare time, he maintains his website (TrevorGrantThomas.com) where he provides Christian commentary and information. His columns have appeared in such publications as American Thinker, Center for a Just Society, Real Clear Religion, Real Clear History, Real Clear Science, U.S. Action News, as well as *The Atlanta Journal-Constitution* and *The Gainesville Times*.

In her spare time, Michelle writes for her website KingdomCrossing.com, handles the finances for their church, works part time from home, edits Trevor's columns, and serves on the board of Gainesville Homeschool Academy. She was campaign manager for her uncle's campaign for U.S. Congress in 2012 and spearheaded the birth of Legacy Homeschool Academy in 2013.

Michelle graduated from North Georgia College in 1995 with a B.S. in sociology. Trevor's degrees include a B.S. in physics and an M.Ed. in mathematics education from North Georgia College, as well as an Ed.S. in mathematics education from the University of Georgia.

39433090R00094

Made in the USA
Charleston, SC
10 March 2015